First World War
and Army of Occupation
War Diary
France, Belgium and Germany

37 DIVISION
Divisional Troops
Royal Army Medical Corps
50 Field Ambulance
10 June 1915 - 30 April 1919

WO95/2526/1

The Naval & Military Press Ltd
www.nmarchive.com
Published in association with The National Archives

Published by

The Naval & Military Press Ltd

Unit 10 Ridgewood Industrial Park,

Uckfield, East Sussex,

TN22 5QE England

Tel: +44 (0) 1825 749494

www.naval-military-press.com

www.nmarchive.com

This diary has been reprinted in facsimile from the original. Any imperfections are inevitably reproduced and the quality may fall short of modern type and cartographic standards.

© **Crown Copyright**
Images reproduced by permission of The National Archives, London, England, 2015.

Contents

Document type	Place/Title	Date From	Date To
Heading	WO95/2526/1 1915 June-1919 Apr 50 Field Amb		
Heading	37th Division Medical 50th Field Ambulance 1915 Jun-1919 Apl		
Heading	37th Division 50th Field Ambulance Vol I June To Oct 15 Aug 15 To Dec 18		
Heading	War Diary of Major A.J. Carlyon R.A.M.C. Officer Commanding No 50 Field Ambulance From 10th June 1915 To 31st October 1915 Volume 1		
War Diary	Llandrindod Wells Wales	10/06/1915	10/06/1915
War Diary	Limerick	11/06/1915	21/06/1915
War Diary	Tidworth	22/06/1915	31/07/1915
War Diary	Havre	01/08/1915	01/08/1915
War Diary	Audricques	02/08/1915	02/08/1915
War Diary	Lostrat	03/08/1915	04/08/1915
War Diary	Arques	05/08/1915	05/08/1915
War Diary	Hazebrook	06/08/1915	20/08/1915
War Diary	St Jans Cappel	21/08/1915	22/08/1915
War Diary	Armentieres	23/08/1915	23/08/1915
War Diary	Hazebrook	24/08/1915	24/08/1915
War Diary	Orville	25/08/1915	05/09/1915
War Diary	Henu	06/09/1915	31/10/1915
Heading	37th Division 50th F.A. Vol. 2 Nov 15		
Heading	War Diary of Major A J Carlyon R.A.M.C. From 1st Nov 1915 To 30 Nov 1915. Vol. 2		
War Diary	Henu	01/11/1915	30/11/1915
Heading	37th Div F/1991 Dec 1915 50th F.a. Vol 3		
War Diary	Henu	01/12/1915	30/12/1915
Heading	50th F.A. Vol 4 Jan 1916		
Heading	War Diary Of Lieut Col. A.F. Carlyon R.A.M.C. from 9th January 1916 to 31st January 1916. Vol 4		
War Diary	Henu	09/01/1916	31/01/1916
Heading	50th Field Ambulance Feb 1916 March		
Heading	War Diary of Lieut Col A.F. Carlyon R.A.M.C. Commanding No 50 Field Ambulance from February 1-1916 to February 29 1916 50th F.A. 37 Div Vol. 5		
War Diary	Henu	01/02/1916	29/02/1916
Heading	War Diary of Lieut Col A.F. Carlyon R.A.M.C. O.C. 50 Field Ambulance From 1 March 1916 to 31st March 1916 Vol 6		
War Diary	Henu	01/03/1916	18/03/1916
War Diary	Haut Visee	19/03/1916	31/03/1916
Heading	War Diary of Lieut Col A.F. Carlyon R.A.M.C. Commanding No 50 Field Ambulance From 1st April 1916 to 30th April 1916 Vol 7		
War Diary	Haut Visee	01/04/1916	30/04/1916
Heading	War Diary of Lieut Col. A.F. Carlyon R.A.M.C. O.C. 50 Field Ambulance from May 1st 1916 to May 31st 1916 Vol 8		
War Diary	Haut Visee	01/05/1916	01/05/1916
War Diary	La Herliere	02/05/1916	31/05/1916

Miscellaneous	From Officer Commanding 50 Field Ambulance	01/07/1916	01/07/1916
Heading	War Diary of Lieut Col A.F. Carlyon R.A.M.C. Officer Commanding No 50 Field Ambulance Up to 27th June 1916 Capt M.W. Paterson Officer Commanding No 50 Field Ambulance From that date From June 1-1916 to June 30-1916. Vol 9		
War Diary	La Herliere	01/06/1916	30/06/1916
Heading	War Diary of M.W. Paterson Capt R.A.M.C. O.C. 50 Field Ambulance from 1 July 1916 to 31 July 1916 (Volume 10)		
War Diary	Laherliere	01/07/1916	03/07/1916
War Diary	Gaudiempre	04/07/1916	13/07/1916
War Diary	Houvin-Houvigneul	14/07/1916	14/07/1916
War Diary	Marquay	15/07/1916	18/07/1916
War Diary	Bruay	19/07/1916	25/07/1916
War Diary	Estree-Cauchie	26/07/1916	31/07/1916
Heading	War Diary of O.C 50th Field Ambulance from 1st August 1916 to 31st August 1916		
War Diary	Estree-Cauchie	01/08/1916	14/08/1916
War Diary	Bruay	14/08/1916	31/08/1916
Heading	War Diary of 50th Field Ambulance. From 1st September 1916 to 30th September 1916. Vol XIV		
War Diary	Bruay	01/09/1916	18/09/1916
War Diary	Barlin	19/09/1916	19/09/1916
War Diary	Barlin	20/09/1916	30/09/1916
War Diary	Bruay		
War Diary	Barlin		
Heading	War Diary of Major T.B. Nicholls R.A.M.C. Commanding 50th Field Ambulance From 1st October 1916 to 31st October 1916 Vol 15		
War Diary	Barlin	01/10/1916	15/10/1916
War Diary	Fresnicourt	16/10/1916	16/10/1916
War Diary	Dieval	17/10/1916	18/10/1916
War Diary	St Michel	19/10/1916	20/10/1916
War Diary	Moncheaux	21/10/1916	21/10/1916
War Diary	Bretel	22/10/1916	22/10/1916
War Diary	Sarton	23/10/1916	23/10/1916
War Diary	Acheux	24/10/1916	25/10/1916
War Diary	Arqueves	28/10/1916	29/10/1916
War Diary	Sarton	30/10/1916	31/10/1916
Heading	War Diary of Major T.B. Nicholls R.A.M.C. Commanding No 50 Field Ambulance From 1 Nov 1916 to 30 Nov 1916 Vol 14		
War Diary	Bretel	01/11/1916	12/11/1916
War Diary	Louvencourt	13/11/1916	15/11/1916
War Diary	Clairfaye	16/11/1916	27/11/1916
War Diary	Louvencourt	28/11/1916	30/11/1916
Miscellaneous	Report of Operations Carried Out by Appendix I Nov 13th 17th 1916		
Miscellaneous	To O.C. 50th Field Ambulance Appendix II	18/11/1916	18/11/1916
Miscellaneous	Report of Operations Carried Out by Appendix II	19/11/1916	19/11/1916
Heading	War Diary of Lieut Col. J.B. Nicholls R.A.M.C. Commanding 50th Field Ambulance from December 1st 1916 to December 31st 1916 (Volume 17)		
War Diary	Val De Maison	01/12/1916	13/12/1916
War Diary	Bretel	14/12/1916	14/12/1916

War Diary	Noeux	15/12/1916	15/12/1916
War Diary	Hericourt	16/12/1916	16/12/1916
War Diary	Pessy Les Pernes	17/12/1916	17/12/1916
War Diary	Norrent Fontes	18/12/1916	18/12/1916
War Diary	Calonne	19/12/1916	20/12/1916
War Diary	Vielle Chapelle	21/12/1916	31/12/1916
Miscellaneous Heading	War Diary of Lieut Col. T.B. Nicholls R.A.M.C. Commanding 50th Field Ambulance from 1st January 1917 to 31st January 1917 (Volume 18)		
War Diary	Vielle Chapelle	01/01/1917	31/01/1917
Heading	War Diary of Lieut. Col. T.B. Nicholls-R.A.M.C. Commanding 50th Field Ambulance. from February 1st 1917 to February 28th 1917. (Volume 19)		
War Diary	Vieille Chapelle	01/02/1917	03/02/1917
War Diary	Calonne-Sur-La-Lys	04/01/1917	10/02/1917
War Diary	Bethune	11/02/1917	12/02/1917
War Diary	Braquemont	13/02/1917	28/02/1917
Heading	War Diary of Officer Commanding 50th Field Ambulance. From 1st March 1917 to 31st March 1917 (Volume 20)		
War Diary	Braquemont	01/03/1917	03/03/1917
War Diary	Bethune	04/03/1917	04/03/1917
War Diary	L'Ecleme	05/03/1917	05/03/1917
War Diary	Nedonchelle	06/03/1917	08/03/1917
War Diary	Valhuon	09/03/1917	09/03/1917
War Diary	Rebreuviette.	10/03/1917	31/03/1917
Heading	War Diary of O.C. 50th Field Ambulance April 1917. Orders by A.D.M.S. 37th Division. Appendix I		
Miscellaneous	Medical Arrangements. 37th Division Operations. No. 27	27/03/1917	27/03/1917
Map			
Heading	War Diary of Officer Commanding 50th Field Ambulance From 1st April 1917 to 30th April 1917. (Volume 21)		
War Diary	Rebreuviette.	01/04/1917	05/04/1917
War Diary	Bellavesnes.	07/04/1917	16/04/1917
War Diary	Habarcq	17/04/1917	21/04/1917
War Diary	St Nicholas.	22/04/1917	22/04/1917
War Diary	St Laurant-Blangy.	22/04/1917	30/04/1917
Operation(al) Order(s)	Instructions to Accompany Medical Arrangements Operations No. 27	02/04/1917	02/04/1917
Operation(al) Order(s)	R.A.M.C. 37th Division. Operation Order No. 28. Supplementary to Order No. 27	03/04/1917	03/04/1917
Heading	War Diary of O.C. 50th Field Ambulance April 1917 Appendix II		
Miscellaneous Map	Bridge Over Fosse From Bastion	31/03/1917	31/03/1917
Miscellaneous	Scheme For Evacuation of Walking Wounded.	27/03/1917	27/03/1917
Miscellaneous	Report On Evacuation of Walking Wounded from Bastion Arras to Warlus By Horse Ambulances.	12/04/1917	12/04/1917
Miscellaneous	Bastion-Wagonlieu-Warlus Routs for Walking Wounded April 9th and 10th 1917	09/04/1917	09/04/1917
Miscellaneous	To O.C., 50th Field Ambulance.	03/04/1917	03/04/1917
Miscellaneous	To, O.C., 50th Field Ambulance.		

Heading	War Diary of O.C. 50th Field Ambulance April 1917 Appendix IV		
Miscellaneous	Report on 8th East Lancs Regimental aid Post during recent Operations.	14/04/1917	14/04/1917
Heading	War Diary of O.C. 50th Field Ambulance April 1917 Appendix V		
Miscellaneous	Alterations in Medical Arrangements Suggested by Operation Commencing 9th April 1917	09/04/1917	09/04/1917
Miscellaneous	The Utilization Of Heat Of Incinerators, by Capt. (Actg. Lt. Col.) T.B. Nicholls. Royal Army Medical Corps.	29/07/1917	29/07/1917
Heading	War Diary of Officer Commanding 50th Field Ambulance From 1st May 1917 to 31st May 1917. (Volume 22)		
War Diary	Ambrines	01/05/1917	18/05/1917
War Diary	Gouves	19/05/1917	19/05/1917
War Diary	Arras.	20/05/1917	30/05/1917
Heading	War Diary of Officer Commanding 50th Field Ambulance from 1st June 1917 to 30th June 1917. (Volume 23.)		
War Diary	Duisans	01/06/1917	03/06/1917
War Diary	Lignereuil	05/06/1917	07/06/1917
War Diary	Belval	08/06/1917	08/06/1917
War Diary	Coyecque	09/06/1917	23/06/1917
War Diary	Wittes.	24/06/1917	24/06/1917
War Diary	Hondeghem.	25/06/1917	25/06/1917
War Diary	Locre.	27/06/1917	28/06/1917
War Diary	Dranoutre.	30/06/1917	30/06/1917
Heading	War Diary of Officer Commanding 50th Field Ambulance from 1st July 1917. to 31st July 1917. (Volume 24.)		
War Diary	Dranoutre	01/07/1917	31/07/1917
Heading	War Diary of Officer Commanding 50th Field Ambulance From 1st August 1917 to 31st August 1917 (Volume 25.)		
War Diary	Dranoutre	01/08/1917	08/08/1917
War Diary	Bailleul	09/08/1917	31/08/1917
War Diary	In The Field	31/08/1917	31/08/1917
Heading	War Diary of Officer Commanding 50th Field Ambulance From 1st September 1917 to 30th September 1917. (Volume 26.)		
War Diary	Bailleul	02/09/1917	30/09/1917
War Diary	In The Field	30/09/1917	30/09/1917
Miscellaneous	Bearer Sub-Divisions.		
Miscellaneous	Drying & Bathroom		
Diagram etc	Diagrammatic Sketch of Drying & Batt Room		
Diagram etc	Fig I		
Heading	War Diary of Officer Commanding 50th Field Ambulance from 1st October 1917 to 31st October 1917. (Volume 27)		
War Diary	Bailleul	01/10/1917	31/10/1917
Heading	War Diary of Officer Commanding 50th Field Ambulance From 1st November 1917 to 30th November 1917 (Volume 28.)		
War Diary	Bailleul	01/11/1917	17/11/1917
War Diary	Magilligan Camp.	20/11/1917	30/11/1917

Heading	War Diary of Officer Commanding 50th Field Ambulance from 1st December 1917 to 31st December 1917 (Volume 29)		
War Diary	Magilligan Camp	03/12/1917	27/12/1917
War Diary	In The Field	31/12/1917	31/12/1917
Heading	War Diary of Officer Commanding 50th Field Ambulance from 1st January 1918 to 31st January 1918 (Volume 30.)		
War Diary	Magilligan Camp.	01/01/1918	11/01/1918
War Diary	Bailleul	13/01/1918	31/01/1918
Heading	War Diary of Officer Commanding 50th Field Ambulance from 1st February 1918 to 28th February 1918 (Volume 31)		
War Diary	Bailleul	01/02/1918	13/02/1918
War Diary	Woodcote House	16/02/1918	28/02/1918
Heading	War Diary of Officer Commanding 50th Field Ambulance from 1st March 1918 to 31st March 1918 (Volume 32)		
War Diary	Woodcote House.	01/03/1918	27/03/1918
War Diary	Waratah Camp	28/03/1918	30/03/1918
War Diary	Marieux	31/03/1918	31/03/1918
Miscellaneous	50th. Field Ambulance.	01/03/1918	01/03/1918
Heading	War Diary of Officer Commanding 50th Field Ambulance from 1st April 1918 to 30th April 1918 (Volume 33)		
War Diary	Humbercamp	01/04/1918	01/04/1918
War Diary	Couin	03/04/1918	17/04/1918
War Diary	Marieux	24/04/1918	25/04/1918
War Diary	Pas-En-Artois	27/04/1918	30/04/1918
Heading	War Diary of Officer Commanding 50th Field Ambulance from 1st May 1918. to 31st May 1918. (Volume 34.)		
War Diary	Pas-En-Artois	01/05/1918	17/05/1918
War Diary	Authie	18/05/1918	31/05/1918
Heading	War Diary of Officer Commanding 50th Field Ambulance From 1st June 1918 30th June 1918 (Volume 35.)		
War Diary	Authie	02/06/1918	06/06/1918
War Diary	St. Pierre-A-Gouy.	10/06/1918	10/06/1918
War Diary	Neuville-Sous-Loevilly.	12/06/1918	21/06/1918
War Diary	Henu	21/06/1918	25/06/1918
War Diary	Bienvillers	28/06/1918	30/06/1918
Heading	War Diary of Officer Commanding 50th Field Ambulance from 1st July 1918 to 31st July 1918 (Volume 36.)		
War Diary	Bienvillers	01/07/1918	31/07/1918
Heading	War Diary of Officer Commanding 50th Field Ambulance from 1st August 1918 to 31st August 1918. (Volume 37.)		
War Diary	Bienvillers	01/08/1918	26/08/1918
War Diary	Achiet-Le-Grand	27/08/1918	31/08/1918
Heading	War Diary Of Officer Commanding 50th Field Ambulance From 1st September 1918 to 30th September 1918 Volume 38		
War Diary	Achiet-Le-Grand	01/09/1918	04/09/1918
War Diary	Lebucquiere	09/09/1918	10/09/1918

War Diary	Bertincourt	11/09/1918	15/09/1918
War Diary	Ruyaulcourt	18/09/1918	21/09/1918
War Diary	Le Barque	22/09/1918	30/09/1918
Heading	War Diary of Officer Commanding 50th Field Ambulance From 1st October 1918 to 31st October 1918 (Volume 39.)		
War Diary	Ytres	01/10/1918	01/10/1918
War Diary	Metz	02/10/1918	06/10/1918
War Diary	Gouzeaucourt	07/10/1918	09/10/1918
War Diary	Vauchelles	10/10/1918	10/10/1918
War Diary	Esnes	10/10/1918	10/10/1918
War Diary	Ligny	11/10/1918	25/10/1918
War Diary	Briastre	28/10/1918	31/10/1918
Heading	War Diary of Officer Commanding 50th Field Ambulance from 1st November 1918 to 30th November 1918 (Volume 40.)		
War Diary	Briastre	04/11/1918	08/11/1918
War Diary	Beaurain	09/11/1918	09/11/1918
War Diary	Louvignies	09/11/1918	11/11/1918
War Diary	Bethencourt	12/11/1918	30/11/1918
Heading	War Diary of Officer Commanding 50th Field Ambulance From 1st December 1918 to 31st December 1918. (Volume 41)		
War Diary	Bethencourt	01/12/1918	01/12/1918
War Diary	Bermerain	02/12/1918	02/12/1918
War Diary	Eth	05/12/1918	14/12/1918
War Diary	Bettrechies	15/12/1918	15/12/1918
War Diary	La Longueville	17/12/1918	17/12/1918
War Diary	Elesmes	18/12/1918	18/12/1918
War Diary	Binche	19/12/1918	19/12/1918
War Diary	Pieton	20/12/1918	20/12/1918
War Diary	Jumet	22/12/1918	31/12/1918
Heading	War Diary of Officer Commanding 50th Field Ambulance from 1st January 1919 to 31st January 1919 (Volume 42)		
War Diary	Jumet (Hamendes)	05/01/1919	31/01/1919
Heading	War Diary of Officer Commanding 50th Field Ambulance from 1st February 1919 to 28th February 1919. (Volume 43)		
War Diary	Jumet (Hamendes)	03/02/1919	28/02/1919
Heading	War Diary of Officer Commanding 50th Field Ambulance from 1st March 1919 to 31st March 1919. (Volume 44)		
War Diary Miscellaneous	Jumet (Hamendes)	03/03/1919	31/03/1919
Heading	War Diary of Officer Commanding 50th Field Ambulance from 1st April 1919 to 30th April 1919 (Volume 45)		
War Diary	Jumet (Hamendes)	04/04/1919	30/04/1919

WO 95
2526/1

1915 June – 1919 Apr
30 Field Amb

37TH DIVISION
MEDICAL

50TH FIELD AMBULANCE
~~AUG 1915 - DEC 1918~~
1915 JUN — 1919 APL

121/7430

37 MKennen

50th Field Ambulance.
Vol: I
June to Oct 15

Aug 15
Dec 18

Confidential

War Diary

of

Major A. F. Carlyon, R.A.M.C.

Officer Commanding No. 50 Field Ambulance

From 10th June 1915 To 31st October 1915

Volume 1

Army Form C. 2118

WAR DIARY
or
INTELLIGENCE SUMMARY

(Erase heading not required.)

Instructions regarding War Diaries and Intelligence Summaries are contained in F. S. Regs., Part II. and the Staff Manual respectively. Title Pages will be prepared in manuscript.

Place	Date	Hour	Summary of Events and Information	Remarks and references to Appendices
LLANDRINDOD WELLS WALES	June 10th		Under orders received from the War Office, I proceeded to LIMERICK to take over command of No 50 Field Ambulance	
LIMERICK	June 11th		Arrived LIMERICK on June 11th. There was no Quartermaster appointed to the Field Ambulance. The transport was complete as regards the horse-drawn vehicles, but there were no horses. There were five other officers besides myself attached to the unit, viz; Lieuts McALDEN, PATERSON, WAY, GOVER, & RODDY are	Arthur Ouigham asst
"	June 12th		I commenced taking over charge of the unit, moved to the War Office for a Quartermaster.	are
"	June 15th		Completed taking over the unit	are
"	June 16th		Received orders to proceed to TIDWORTH to join 3rd Division 2nd Army Corps.	are

Army Form C. 2118

WAR DIARY
or
INTELLIGENCE SUMMARY
(Erase heading not required.)

Instructions regarding War Diaries and Intelligence Summaries are contained in F. S. Regs., Part II. and the Staff Manual respectively. Title Pages will be prepared in manuscript.

Place	Date	Hour	Summary of Events and Information	Remarks and references to Appendices
LIMERICK	June 23rd		Left LIMERICK for TIDWORTH travelling via ROSSLARE & FISHGUARD at Tidworth Camp Hants	
TIDWORTH	June 24th		Arrived TIDWORTH at 7am. Found our horses for transport awaiting us there. Quartered in TIDWORTH PARK CAMP. a/c	
"	June 25th		A. D. M. S., 37th Division inspected Coy a/c	
"	June 26th		Route march in the morning. a/c	
"	June 27th		Unpacked wagons & practised repacking them; am. Lecture on 'care of feet' etc. to personnel in the afternoon.	
"	June 28th		Unit field training a/c	
"	June 29th		Unit field training a/c	
"	June 29th		Unit field training a/c	
"	June 30th		Unit field training. am	

Army Form C. 2118

WAR DIARY
or
INTELLIGENCE SUMMARY
(Erase heading not required.)

Instructions regarding War Diaries and Intelligence Summaries are contained in F. S. Regs., Part II. and the Staff Manual respectively. Title Pages will be prepared in manuscript.

Place	Date	Hour	Summary of Events and Information	Remarks and references to Appendices
TIDWORTH	July 1st		Unit field training. Lectures ong Rlinic	
	July 2nd		Unit field training. AYC	
	July 3rd		Route march in the morning. AYC	
	July 5th		Unit field training, O/C MacRAE, MACFARLANE, CAMPBELL joined for duty, AYC	
	July 6th		Lieut. Quartermaster COLAHAN joined for duty. AYC	
	July 7th		Unit field training. AYC	
	July 8th		Route march in the morning – Lectures to personnel in the afternoon AYC	
	July 9th		Unit field training. AYC	
	July 10th		Route march in the morning. AYC	
	July 12th		Unit field training. AYC	
	July 13th		Route march in morning. Unloaded & repacked wagons in the afternoon. AYC	
	July 14th		Route march in the morning. Lectures to personnel in the afternoon AYC	
	July 15th		Unit field training. AYC	
	July 16th		Unit field training. AYC	

1875 Wt. W593/826 1,000,000 4/15 J.B.C. & A. A.D.S.S./Forms/C. 2118.

Army Form C. 2118

WAR DIARY
or
INTELLIGENCE SUMMARY

(Erase heading not required.)

Instructions regarding War Diaries and Intelligence Summaries are contained in F.S. Regs., Part II. and the Staff Manual respectively. Title Pages will be prepared in manuscript.

Place	Date	Hour	Summary of Events and Information	Remarks and references to Appendices
TIDWORTH	July 17th		Divisional manoeuvres. Orders for Route March	
	July 18th		Unit field training	am
	July 20th		Route march in morning, lectures to personnel in afternoon	am
	July 21st		Way or drill in the morning. Searching wounded by night 9-11pm one	
	July 22nd		Work could be carried out in the field out to the wet weather but lectures were given to two hours in the morning, two in the afternoon or	
	July 23rd		weather too inclement, out lectures could be given during the day	am
	August 1st		Route march in the morning — lectures in the afternoon	am
	July 11th		Unit received orders to embark for FRANCE on 30th inst.	am
	July 27th		Started getting ready to move — fixed some of the wagons	am
	July 9th		Continued preparations for the move — also see details	am
	July 29th		Final preparation for move completed. See details and to SLING CAMP	are
	July 30th		Left TIDWORTH 11:10 am to SOUTHAMPTON. Embarked on "VITER" as regards personnel, transport horses but on another ship.	and
	July 30th		Arrived HAVRE 7:20 am disembarked 7:30 am. Transport arrived at Havre 9:10pm until nearly 4pm to get everything disembarked. Personnel though remained in the docks for the night. Very unsatisfactory accommodation.	are

WAR DIARY
or
INTELLIGENCE SUMMARY

(Erase heading not required.)

Army Form C. 2118

Place	Date	Hour	Summary of Events and Information	Remarks and references to Appendices
HAVRE	August 1st		Entrained at 1.45 pm for an unknown destination. O.C./p/Sm. Reeve	
AUDRICQUES	Aug 2nd		Arrived AUDRICQUES at 7am. after disentraining we marched to LOSTRAT. Officers & men billeted at different farms in the district.	A.H.C.
LOSTRAT	Aug 3rd		Weather very unfavourable. A.D.M.S. 27 Division came to see us, also Brigadier General	A.H.C.
LOSTRAT	Aug 4th		Left LOSTRAT at 7am in fine weather. Arrived TILQUES 1.30 where lunch had midday meal & then marched on to ARQUES arriving about 6pm. Officers & men billeted in farms.	A.H.C
ARQUES	Aug 5th		Left ARQUES at 7.45 am. Arrived HAZEBROUCK 3 o'clock. Officers & men billeted at la ferme before. Motor Ambulances by Wheeler (4,3 Forby) + 1 motor cycle with personnel joined the unit.	A.H.C
HAZEBROUCK	Aug 6th		A.D.M.S. to see us. Also W/L EVANS D.S.O. R.A.M.C. Inspected our motor ambulances.	A.H.C

Army Form C. 2118

WAR DIARY
or
INTELLIGENCE SUMMARY
(Erase heading not required.)

Instructions regarding War Diaries and Intelligence Summaries are contained in F. S. Regs., Part II. and the Staff Manual respectively. Title Pages will be prepared in manuscript.

Place	Date	Hour	Summary of Events and Information	Remarks and references to Appendices
HAZEBROOK	Aug 8		Went out to CASTRE to see A.D.M.S. — CASTRE being Divisional Headquarters. Personnel unloaded wagons, prepared them in the morning, bathing parade in the afternoon. Water has to be fetched from a stream about 1 mile away as the farm pump is beginning to run dry.	a/c afterpart
"	Aug 9		Inspection by General PLUMER at 11 a.m.	a/c
"	Aug 10		Sick to be evacuated to No 15 C.C. Station. Went down with two cases in the morning. Bathing parade in the afternoon.	a/c HAZEBROOK
"	Aug 10th		Went out to CASTRE to see A.D.M.S. Route march to hurst in morning. Bathing parade in afternoon.	a/c
"	Aug 11th		Went into CASTRE to get money for personnel. Field Ambulance drill in morning. Bathing parade in afternoon. Paid Recruitmen at 5 p.m.	a/c

1875 Wt. W593/826 1,000,000 4/15 J.B.C. & A. A.D.S.S./Forms/C. 2118.

WAR DIARY or INTELLIGENCE SUMMARY

Army Form C. 2118

(Erase heading not required.)

Place	Date	Hour	Summary of Events and Information	Remarks and references to Appendices
HAZEBROUCK	Aug 13		Inspection by A.D.M.S. Bathing parade in the afternoon. Nearly dry weather.	
"	Aug 14		Route march in the morning. Lecture to personnel in afternoon. WC	
"	Aug 15		Unloaded & reloaded wagons — oiled woodwork of wagons replenished grease boxes. Bathing parade in the afternoon. WC	
"	Aug 16		Went out to C.A.S.T.R.E to get move for detachments. WC. Route march in morning — tea with afternoon — lecture to personnel by officers to personnel.	
"	Aug 17		Weather very unfavourable. Lecture to officers & personnel morning & afternoon. WC	
"	Aug 18		Weather again very bad. Lectures to personnel by Sergt of section. WC	
"	Aug 19		Went to Castre to draw money for unit. Revd A.L.C. Hine R.C. C.F. joined the unit. ALH	

Army Form C. 2118

WAR DIARY
or
INTELLIGENCE SUMMARY
(Erase heading not required.)

Instructions regarding War Diaries and Intelligence Summaries are contained in F. S. Regs., Part II. and the Staff Manual respectively. Title Pages will be prepared in manuscript.

Place	Date	Hour	Summary of Events and Information	Remarks and references to Appendices
HAZEBROOK	Aug 18		Orders received to change our billets to the other side of HAZEBROOK. Went after tea to find some with Interpreter Rapt WKP. found a billet in a field, after much search for a place with mounted for a first experience, but all the other billets had already been taken up by Infantry Regts etc = Northumbrian Howr —	
HAZEBROOK	Aug 20		Left HAZEBROOK under instruction from A.D.M.S. to undergo a course of instruction for 2 days at St JANS CAPPEL with 20 men. reported myself on arrival to O.C. 1st Northumbrian F.A. T.F. Went round the camp in the morning, saw several points of interest including latrines etc. Went into BALLIEUL in the afternoon.	a/c
"			Continued receiving instruction.	a/c
ST JANS CAPPEL	Aug 22		Left St JANS CAPPEL & proceeded to ARMENTIÈRES for further instructions. reported myself to O.C. 3rd Northumbrian F.A. T.F. Went round the Old Asile station with the O.C. & with HOUPLINES in the evening.	a/c

WAR DIARY or INTELLIGENCE SUMMARY

Army Form C. 2118

(Erase heading not required.)

Place	Date	Hour	Summary of Events and Information	Remarks and references to Appendices
ARMENTIERES	Aug 1st 15		Continued receiving instruction in various matters	unfortunately [illegible]
HAZEBROUCK	Aug 2nd		Left to return to HAZEBROOK. On our arrival there found orders waiting for the Unit to proceed to ORVILLE. Started packing wagons etc	are
ORVILLE	Aug 3rd		Left HAZEBROOK at 4 a.m. marched to CASSEL + entrained there for MONDICOURT where we detrained + marched to ORVILLE. Again the place chosen for the Field Ambulance was a most unsatisfactory one + quite unsuited to a place to treat sick.	are
"	Aug 4th		Motored into DOULLENS to see A.D.M.S. G.O.C. 2nd Army came to see us about 4 p.m.	are

WAR DIARY
or
INTELLIGENCE SUMMARY

(Erase heading not required.)

Army Form C. 2118

Place	Date	Hour	Summary of Events and Information	Remarks and references to Appendices
BRNVILLE	Aug 26		Took sick LtCol & Casualty Clearing Station at BEAUVAL. Weather very unfavourable. Rate of Casu[alti]es a quagmire. Wagons bogged down.	
"	Aug 27		Weather again very inclement. Personnel very uncomfortable. Sleeping under waterproof sheets without blankets. etc.	
"	Aug 28		Orders received to prepare for another move. Started packing up equipment etc.	
"	Aug 29		Motored to HENU. Chose a site for dressing station. to TONGVILLERS where a ruined house at present occupied by french. I stated post was chosen for advanced dressing station as steel food bomb proof shelters where the sick & wounded could be put if necessary.	
"	Aug 30		Went the same round as yesterday with A.D.M.S.	WL

WAR DIARY
or
INTELLIGENCE SUMMARY

(Erase heading not required.)

Army Form C. 2118

Instructions regarding War Diaries and Intelligence Summaries are contained in F. S. Regs., Part II. and the Staff Manual respectively. Title Pages will be prepared in manuscript.

Place	Date	Hour	Summary of Events and Information	Remarks and references to Appendices
ORVILLE	Sept 1st		Went with Major OXLEY in car for detachment. Finished packing equipment & ready for a move. Weather for week — rather showery.	
ORVILLE	Sept 2nd		Advance party to go to FONQUEVILLERS from advanced dressing station tomorrow. Raining hard all day. Went with DOYLE NSS to see ADMS.	
"	Sept 3rd		Went & left for ORVILLE at 9am with Capt PATERSON & 20 men to form the advanced dressing station at FONQUEVILLERS. When we got there found that the place chosen previously belonged to 48 Division so had to find another. With great difficulty found a place further up in the village. Left Capt PATERSON there the men with one motor ambulance. A journal service wagon returned arriving to ORVILLE etc. are	
"	Sept 4th		Received orders for him to move to HENU tomorrow to form dressing station. Another very wet day.	

1875 Wt. W593/826 1,000,000 4/15 J.B.C. & A. A.D.S.S./Forms/C. 2113.

WAR DIARY or INTELLIGENCE SUMMARY

Army Form C. 2118

Place	Date	Hour	Summary of Events and Information	Remarks and references to Appendices
ORVILLE	Sept 5th		Left ORVILLE at dawn – marched to HENU – started getting the Chateau ready for reception of sick & wounded – whole building scrubbed out & first taking – dug etc. – weather very poor.	
HENU	Sept 6th		Continued getting the place ready. Hun with PAS took a Bn Salvoir reconnaissance. An ready to receive sick – a few cases admitted today. AMC	
"	Sept 7th		Col SWAN. D.D.M.S. 3rd Division came out to see us – Put up all our huts to accommodation & wounded – moved officers of the unit to the top floor of the building – can now accommodate 100 sick. AMC Brigadier General came to see us in the afternoon.	
"	Sept 8th		Ordered to send all huts into divisional Rest Station at PAS, then known to accommodation very considerable. Col ALEXIS THOMSON RAMC (Consulting Surgeon) came to see us. AMC Capt PATERSON returned from advanced dressing station & Capt McCAUDEN relieved him.	

Army Form C. 2118.

WAR DIARY
or
INTELLIGENCE SUMMARY.
(Erase heading not required.)

Instructions regarding War Diaries and Intelligence Summaries are contained in F.S. Regs., Part II. and the Staff Manual respectively. Title pages will be prepared in manuscript.

Hour, Date, Place	Summary of Events and Information	Remarks and references to Appendices
HENO Sept 9th	Went into PAS in the morning to fetch for M. detachment.	
"	General Count Gleichen (from N 3) H Division inspected us in the afternoon — Went out to advanced dressing station at FONQUIVILLERS after dark & found all correct arrangements one hour	
" Sept 10th	Surg. Genl. Treherne inspected us in the morning. Spent the afternoon whitewashing kitchen, store etc.	
" Sept 11th	Filled our palliasse pillow cases with chaff. Turned out Quartermasters store, whitewashed it & turned it into a ward.	o.c.
" Sept 12th	Sunday.	
" Sept 13th	A motor ambulance sent to BIENVILLERS (to be relieved daily) so that they is required by 4 9 F.A.	

Army Form C. 2118.

WAR DIARY
or
INTELLIGENCE SUMMARY.
(Erase heading not required.)

Instructions regarding War Diaries and Intelligence Summaries are contained in F.S. Regs., Part II. and the Staff Manual respectively. Title pages will be prepared in manuscript.

Hour, Date, Place	Summary of Events and Information	Remarks and references to Appendices

HENU Sept 13th (contd) in evacuating the sick + wounded that I had at our disposal. Started away by train.

" Sept 14th Went out to BIENVILLERS with Maj. AHERNE near to have a site for another advanced dressing station shewn to he required one. In discussing proposed system for evacuation rather of the instructions from A.D.M.S. times.
received to stop sending motor ambulances to BIENVILLERS such sick and into civil hospital at DOULLENS. AIL.

" Sept 15th

" Sept 16th Naval hospital brought in in the morning. Stretcher drill over obstacle. Lectures to personnel in the afternoon. are

" Sept 17th Went into P.S. three C.R.E. about the state of stretchers in the morning. A.I.C.

WAR DIARY
or
INTELLIGENCE SUMMARY.
(Erase heading not required.)

Army Form C. 2118.

Hour, Date, Place	Summary of Events and Information	Remarks and references to Appendices
HENO Sept 18th	A.D.M.S. Self went to OP for new advanced dressing station instead of the first to no villages as the latter is rendered too exposed to fire. Have decided that a dug out wd.ne used & made about half a mile behind the present advd. Dr. Station.	
" Sep 19/15	Motored to NOVELLE & Suttlofs 9A.T. & 800 car to the F.C 15 & O.R.F about building a well. Hugon to Co. he promised 50 doors and possible. Removed a order of 9th Equipment Coy for ON BULLETS in crock. No more here. My the sudden.	
" Sept 20th	Went into PAS to see A.D.M.S about reserve matters. Hospital routine as usual Ore.	

Army Form C. 2118.

WAR DIARY
or
INTELLIGENCE SUMMARY.
(Erase heading not required.)

Instructions regarding War Diaries and Intelligence Summaries are contained in F. S. Regs., Part II. and the Staff Manual respectively. Title pages will be prepared in manuscript.

Hour, Date, Place	Summary of Events and Information	Remarks and references to Appendices
HENU Sept 21st	Pte Knowles 8869 Lancs. died at 10am. He was admitted yesterday suffering from fracture of wound of abdomen. He was buried at 7pm in the cemetery at HENU. Went out to 9 officers with 2 M.S. & 9 S trumpets advanced dressing station —	
" Sept 22nd	Usual hospital routine all day.	
" Sept 23rd	Orders received to be prepared for a possible sudden move. Stretcher bearer subdivision all equipped for instant start + Officer warned to be ready. — Heavy shelling of enemy trenches began in the evening + continued all day.	
" Sept 24th	A.D.M.S. came in the afternoon + sent out to advanced dressing station in the evening Rumour to the effect that we had two been through	
" Sept 25th	the enemy line. Shelling kept up on both sides.	
" Sept 26th	Usual hospital routine	

WAR DIARY
or
INTELLIGENCE SUMMARY.
(Erase heading not required.)

Army Form C. 2118.

Hour, Date, Place	Summary of Events and Information	Remarks and references to Appendices
#ENO Sept 27th	Usual hospital Routine. Inspection by #D.M.S. 5th Division afterwards by Major Reilly	
" Sept 28th	Usual hospital routine. Red X Society brought fruit & other gifts to patients. AMC	
" Sept 29th	Very inclement weather - turn out to advanced dressing station at Foncquevillers in the evening, everything quiet AMC	
" Sept 30th	Usual hospital routine. German aeroplane passed over the chateau, fly very low. AMC	
" Oct 1st	Sanitary inspection of artillery lines by #ENO in company of M.O.'s. Inspected the new tube helmets from central stores - these were returned at once to D.A.D.M.S. AMC	
" Oct 2nd	Inspected transport lines. Usual hospital Routine. AMC	

WAR DIARY
or
INTELLIGENCE SUMMARY.

(Erase heading not required.)

Army Form C. 2118.

Hour, Date, Place	Summary of Events and Information	Remarks and references to Appendices
HENU Oct 3rd	Usual Sunday Conference in the afternoon at A.D.M.S. Office. P.A.S.	
" Oct 4th	About 7.30 p.m. the body of Pte. McRea No. 60617 15 Co. R.E. was brought to this ambulance in a F.A.M. The M.O. in charge of the unit appeared a bit unwilling to sign a death certificate. The case was one of probable flour [ptomaine?] poisoning with great congestion of the surrounding parts. In fact the bowel was almost gangrenous. The other 8 cases were normal. A.9.Lg	
" Oct 5th	Usual hospital routine carried out.	
" Oct 6th	D.M.S. 37 Division made an inspection in the afternoon. A.Y.C.	

WAR DIARY
or
INTELLIGENCE SUMMARY.
(Erase heading not required.)

Army Form C. 2118.

Hour, Date, Place	Summary of Events and Information	Remarks and references to Appendices
H.Q. Nov. Oct 7th	Usual hospital routine in the morning. A.D.M.S. 37 Division made an inspection. Went out to advanced dressing station in the evening.	
" Oct 8th	Inspection of 125th Bde R.F.A. billets etc at H.F.K.O	
" Oct 9th	Went over the North portion of the Sector of 125 Bde R.F.A. Sanitary inspection of the camp, billets etc of Reserve of H.F.K.O. Inspected horse lines. Went down to P.A.S. Conference with A.D.M.S. are in the afternoon	
" Oct 11th	Usual hospital routine in morning. Went out to advanced dressing station in the evening	

Army Form C. 2118.

WAR DIARY
or
INTELLIGENCE SUMMARY.
(Erase heading not required.)

Instructions regarding War Diaries and Intelligence Summaries are contained in F.S. Regs., Part II. and the Staff Manual respectively. Title pages will be prepared in manuscript.

Hour, Date, Place	Summary of Events and Information	Remarks and references to Appendices
HENU Oct 12th	Went to BIENVILLERS, BERLES AU BOIS, & HUMBERCAMP with Major Aherne Moore. Of 49 Field Ambulance to see the advanced dressing stations, the dressing station at these places.	another 9 Rams
" Oct 13th	Went to MONDICOURT to see the divisional Rest Station run by No 48 Field Ambulance.	A.H.
" Oct 14th	Weather very bad, no Corps drills or sick calls held, lectures given to orderlies by OCs sections. be close	A.H.
" Oct 15th	Went out to advanced dressing station in the evening	A.H.
" Oct 16th	Paid the personnel	A.H.
" Oct 17th	Weekly conference at A.D.M.S. Office in the afternoon.	A.H.

Army Form C. 2118.

WAR DIARY
or
INTELLIGENCE SUMMARY.
(Erase heading not required.)

Instructions regarding War Diaries and Intelligence Summaries are contained in F.S. Regs., Part II and the Staff Manual respectively. Title pages will be prepared in manuscript.

Hour, Date, Place	Summary of Events and Information	Remarks and references to Appendices
HENU October 8th	Inspection by ADMS 37th Division. Went out to advanced dressing station in the evening. Arrived at Rouge Maison	
" Oct 19th	Moved hospital & routine into the morning. Went down to DAS to see who divisional baths. in the evening.	A.C.
" "	for all horses & mules under cover in barn	A.C.
" Oct 21st	Dolsparks & the Officer F.A. had lumbs of shrapnel of their hand severely damaged advanced dressing station while I was every of sent out to bomb. Was sent out to C.C.S. at once. Went out to advanced dressing station in the evening	A.C.
" Oct 22nd	A.D.M.S came up in the morning. He is to round the lines Drs BENZ & HENU in the afternoon.	A.C.

WAR DIARY
or
INTELLIGENCE SUMMARY.
(Erase heading not required.)

Army Form C. 2118.

Hour, Date, Place	Summary of Events and Information	Remarks and references to Appendices
AEN U Oct 23rd	Inspection by ADMS 37 Division of R.F.A bullets & men at HE NU. Divisional band played in the grounds of the Chateau in the afternoon. Went out to advanced dressing station in the evening. Asylum anywhere	
" Oct 24th	Conference at ADMS. office	
" Oct 25th	ADMS came up in the morning. We inspected the advanced dressing station in the evening.	
" Oct 26th	Started a class on massage for the nursing section. Sgt Macfarlane in charge. ADC	
" Oct 27th	Rest day. No stretcher drill, lecture, to personnel instead. ADC	
" Oct 28th	ADMS came up. Official news that we are warned to proceed after two months relaxation. There are	

Army Form C. 2118.

WAR DIARY
or
INTELLIGENCE SUMMARY.
(*Erase heading not required.*)

Hour, Date, Place	Summary of Events and Information	Remarks and references to Appendices
Reno Oct 29th	Conference at A & M S Office re disposal of sick. Went to advanced dressing station in the evening arranged arrangements	
" Oct 30th	Col. Alexis Thompson (Consulting Surgeon) came round over the field ambulance. D.G.	
" Oct 31st	A very wet day – Church parade in the morning. Conference at A & M S. Office in the afternoon. AGC	

Nov. 1415.

3'7 M. Kwiecin 121/1621

121/1621

1694/7621

Jok F. a.
vol 2

Nov 15

VOL. 2

Confidential

War Diary.

of

Major A. F. Carlyon R.A.M.C

From 1st Nov. 1915   To 30 Nov. 1915

WAR DIARY or INTELLIGENCE SUMMARY

Army Form C. 2118.

Hour, Date, Place	Summary of Events and Information	Remarks and references to Appendices
HENO Nov 1st	Very inclement weather, between divine service and afternoon. Instead of intended drill in the afternoon marched drovers to outrunts evening.	A.F.Brown V.G.Rame
" Nov 2nd	Very cold weather all day. Lectures given instead of drill.	A.F.E
" Nov 3rd	A & An S came round in the morning. Requested to add 15th & 17th to draft to till to be sent up for 2nd class 9th labour battn. who are literated marines by saddecadem in France.	A.F.E
11.00 " 4th	Went into PAS to draw money for personal use also for cylinders of oxygen, rubber bags — also to A.H.Q. only to hear that there is not much likelihood, as we are that number shortly will, first case of "Trench foot" attr. that today.	A.F.E
" Nov 5th	Lt. Trachse leaves for duty with 26 Battalion in accordance with instruction received from A.D.M.S 2nd Division	A.F.E

WAR DIARY
or
INTELLIGENCE SUMMARY.
(Erase heading not required.)

Army Form C. 2118.

Hour, Date, Place	Summary of Events and Information	Remarks and references to Appendices
NENU Nov 6th	At 9 P.M. S came up to see one. Latterly had buried came here at 8 & poured the Chateau thoroughly to safeguard. Went to advanced dressing station in the evening.	
" Nov 7th	Sunday. Divisional band played in the Chateau courtyard in the afternoon & c.	at Nampoel Maname
" "	Received stores from A.D.M.S. for warming billets the Personnel. Inspected billets. Went out to HUMBERCAMP P. in afternoon & see A.D.S.-a. Went out to advanced dressing station in the evening.	
" 9th	Preliminary meeting Divisional Q mas entertainment etc for the personnel etc.	

WAR DIARY
or
INTELLIGENCE SUMMARY.
(Erase heading not required.)

Army Form C. 2118.

Hour, Date, Place	Summary of Events and Information	Remarks and references to Appendices
HENO Nov 10th	Rect of Red X Society representative seeking a list of requirements. Went down to P.A.G in evening. Free A.D.M.S. at Marshy House	
" Nov 11th	A lot of fifty from Red X Soceity arrived at MACFAR & HOUSE. Sent to relieve the M.O. 1/2 g Staffs. proceeding on leave. Went out to advanced dressing station in the evening. ADl.	
" Nov 12th	C.O Inquired into the mental condition of officers on leave.	
	T.C 49 7A came up to Ace One. Ole	
" Nov 13th	Very wet weather. No stretcher drill. Lectures to personnel instead. ADl.	
" Nov 14th	Sunday. Parade Service in the morning. Went out to advanced dressing station. ADl.	

WAR DIARY
or
INTELLIGENCE SUMMARY.

(Erase heading not required.)

Army Form C. 2118.

Hour, Date, Place	Summary of Events and Information	Remarks and references to Appendices

AENO Nov 15th   First fall of snow. Went down to PAS tree ADMS. urban grains

" Nov 16th   ADMS tore arm in the morning. very heavy fall of snow during the night, roads almost impossible for motor cars — Divisional Band played in the afternoon a.D.C.

" Nov 17th   Capt GOVER Royce proceed to GUADIAMPRE for temporary duty. Admitted the sergeant (?) in the evening A.D.C.

" Nov 18th   Went down to PAS in the morning for detachment — paid out in the afternoon a.D.C.

" Nov 19th   A.D.M.S. came up in the morning. Col Swan RDMS 7th Corps also came up three hospital. Summer stores received from ADMS. for A.D.S. WR.

WAR DIARY
or
INTELLIGENCE SUMMARY.
(Erase heading not required.)

Army Form C. 2118.

Hour, Date, Place	Summary of Events and Information	Remarks and references to Appendices
HÉNU Nov 26th	Admiral Sclater came round to see the Chateau this mg. WATSON Rouse in the evening, after inspecting everything here, & took him out to the O.P.S. A.J.W.	
Nov 21st	Capt WAY proceeded on 8 days leave to England — went out to HUMBERCAMP in the afternoon to see I.C.S. Ingram & instructed 4 R.D.M.S. SKevening. A.J.C.	
Nov 22nd	Revd Brennan C.F attached to the ricol ambulance admitted today. McFARLANE returned from 10 days leave. Instr. 11 Suffolks. Went out to Advanced Dressing Station in the evening. A.J.C	
Nov 23rd	Revd Brennan evacuated to C.C.S. Red Cross Society called re Gramaphone etc are.	
Nov 24th	Usual hospital routine. Lecture to orderlies in afternoon on Cleanliness in the Wards etc. Went out to Advanced Dressing Station in the evening. A.J.C	

WAR DIARY
or
INTELLIGENCE SUMMARY.

Army Form C. 2118.

Hour, Date, Place	Summary of Events and Information	Remarks and references to Appendices
HENO Nov 25th	Went down to PAS to see a R.H.S in the morning to Hawford. Lectures to personnel in the afternoon.	
" Nov 26th	Capt GOVER returned from BAUDIMPRE. Went out to advanced Dressing Station in the evening. Artillery Very Heavy. A.T.C.	
" Nov 27th	A.K.M.S came up in the morning. A.T.C Usual Hospital routine. Capt RODY took over duties half & half with the Brigade running an outpatient outdoor.	
" Nov 28th	Capt WATTERSON proceeded on a week's leave to England. A.T.C	
" Nov 29th	Medical Board on 2nd/Lt WHISH R.F.A. Capt WAY returned from leave. A.T.C	
" Nov 30th	Lecture from S.A.M.S 3rd Division — Inspection of tills A.T.C	

37th Div.

50th F.A.
Vol: 3

F/1991

Dec 1915

WAR DIARY
or
INTELLIGENCE SUMMARY.
(Erase heading not required.)

Army Form C. 2118.

Hour, Date, Place	Summary of Events and Information	Remarks and references to Appendices
HENU Section	Revd A.J. Hicks-Gower C.F. arrived for duty. Lectures to orderlies in the afternoon.	A/Major sig Reeves
Dec 2nd	Went to DADS to draw pay for personnel. Saw D.A.D.M.S. Lectures to orderlies in the afternoon.	AJE
Dec 3rd	Three officers arrived from No. 98 Field Ambulance 30th Division for instructional purposes.	AJE
Dec 4th	Went with A.M.E.Ns with an eye case & also to inquire into pieces of food for Xmas Bar dinner for personnel.	AJE
Dec 5th	Sunday. Church parade at 10 am	AJE

Army Form C. 2118.

WAR DIARY
or
INTELLIGENCE SUMMARY.
(Erase heading not required.)

Instructions regarding War Diaries and Intelligence Summaries are contained in F. S. Regs., Part II and the Staff Manual respectively. Title pages will be prepared in manuscript.

Hour, Date, Place	Summary of Events and Information	Remarks and references to Appendices
#ENU Dec 6th	One of the officers from 98 F.A.(T) put under observation for drunkenness at the advanced dressing station F.Y.C. Gunner D. ? taken to Major Rouse, operator for treatment and sent in to HQ 983 Hours. A&C A&C for trying him	
" Dec 7th	General Rouse flying to the station Mess. Capt Patterson returned from leave. A&C Lectures to orderlies	
" Dec 8th	Capt Roddy returned from temporary duty on S.? O/c 1st Rifle Brigade. Very inclement weather - lectures to orderlies in afternoon. A&C	
" Dec 9th	Q.M. to 5 Bn ? Div made an inspection A&C	
" Dec 10th	Col Stevens & 3 officers from 98 F.A. arrived. Two oth officers arrived & unit left, Capt Stephen under orders remain behind ?	
" Nov 5 11th	Col. Stevens returned ?? & took Capt Stephen back with him. The R.C. Chaplain left the R.A. He rewrite the 9th ?? A&C	
" Dec 12th	Lt Campbell leave for ? duty until 10th Royal North Lancs. utility ? Own Sh a 10 to leave A&C	
" Dec 13th	Ried & ? ? to ? to the ? Capt Roddy to be CA himself to ?? for duty with 32 ? A&C	

WAR DIARY
or
INTELLIGENCE SUMMARY.
(Erase heading not required.)

Army Form C. 2118.

Hour, Date, Place	Summary of Events and Information	Remarks and references to Appendices
HENU Dec 15/14/15	Capt RODDY left for duty with 32nd Division. Sent from A & M.S. 37th Division from leave. Capt Greenwood from returned from leave.	Alexander Mr. Ashenbury
" 15th	Capt Green left for duty with 30th Division. Visit from a & M.S. 33rd Division. A dead officer brought to D.O. from Hannescamps. Cause of death found to be ?shell— A.R.C.	
" 16th	Went down to 9AB with motor to draw gowns for Reserved & took them in the afternoon — Lt BRYSON RAMC arrived for duty from 96(S.C.) F.A. Body & stories brought in from Fanceaumps. cause of death suffered mangyum ? ayrds — A.R.C.	
" 17th	Lieut Hew Officers arrived from 97BC (?) F.A. for instruction. Who two whose claims last week are left—	
" 19th	Conference at a & M.S. Office in the afternoon regarding disposal of dental cases. A.R.C.	

Army Form C. 2118.

WAR DIARY
or
INTELLIGENCE SUMMARY.
(Erase heading not required.)

Instructions regarding War Diaries and Intelligence Summaries are contained in F.S. Regs., Part II and the Staff Manual respectively. Title pages will be prepared in manuscript.

Hour, Date, Place	Summary of Events and Information	Remarks and references to Appendices
ENO Dec 1915	Sunday. Church parade in the morning. Lieut. Hindley gave his report that during the heavy shelling of HANNESCAMPS on 17th inst. the promptness & courage under fire of No. 2 05.5079 Pte Wellman A.J. of T.A.S.C. was quite remarkable. The report was passed to A.D.M.S. 37 Division.	
Dec 20th	Capt. M. Allen takes over medical charge of Division whilst there two poor have. Finished Bandages, etc afternoon. Went to Divisional Station att.	
Dec 21st	J.S.M.S. 37 Division came up to see the new Ambulance Hospital one.	
Dec 22nd	Lieut. Hills to the Advanced Dressing Station. morning one	
Dec 23rd	16 rank & file returned from 10 December. Went to GAS w. morning Lere A.D.M.S off.	
Dec 24th	A.D.M.S. came up to see one. Went to HUMBERCAMP in the afternoon.	
Dec 25th	Xmas comforts for the personnel. Smoky Concert in the evening.	
Dec 26th	Sunday. Church parade in the morning.	

WAR DIARY or INTELLIGENCE SUMMARY

Army Form C. 2118

Place	Date	Hour	Summary of Events and Information	Remarks and references to Appendices
Havre	Dec 27th		Went out to Advanced Dressing Station. A/Lt Col Ing Rawe O/C	
"	Dec 28th		A.D.M.S came to make an inspection O/C	
"	Dec 29th		Went to FIENVILLERS with Dr McFarlane to give evidence at the courtmartial of Capt Stephens Rawe. Left HENU at 7 am + did not get back until 9 pm.	
"	Dec 30th		Left HENU at 5.15 am for 8 days leave to ENGLAND travelling via HAVRE + SOUTHAMPTON. Handed over charge to Capt PATTERSON Rawe (SR)	

A.S. Parker
Lt Col
Cmg Rawe

37

Sö. 7. a.
rst. 4

F/1991/2

Jan 1916

Confidential

War Diary

of

Lieut. Col. A. F. Carlyon R.A.M.C

From 9th January 1916 To 31st January 1916

Vol. 4.

Army Form C. 2118.

WAR DIARY
or
INTELLIGENCE SUMMARY.
(Erase heading not required.)

Instructions regarding War Diaries and Intelligence Summaries are contained in F. S. Regs., Part II. and the Staff Manual respectively. Title pages will be prepared in manuscript.

Hour, Date, Place	Summary of Events and Information	Remarks and references to Appendices
HENU Jany 9th 1916	Returned from leave to England. Took over charge & fired ambulance going from Capt Oldham at Cambridge.	
" Jany 10th	Went out to advanced dressing station in the morning. A & M.S. 33 Division came to A.D. in the evening. A&E	
" Jany 11th	A.D.M.S. 37 Division came up in the morning. Usual hospital routine. A&E	
" Jany 12th	Lecture to orderlies on nursing duties in the morning. Visited advanced dressing station in the afternoon. A&E	
" Jany 13th	Went to CHIPILLY write to give evidence at the re-trial of Capt Stephens R.A.M.C. A&E	
" Jany 14th	A.D.M.S. came up in the morning. Visited advanced dressing station in the evening. A&E	

WAR DIARY
or
INTELLIGENCE SUMMARY.
(Erase heading not required.)

Army Form C. 2118.

Hour, Date, Place	Summary of Events and Information	Remarks and references to Appendices
HENU Jan 15th	A very wet day. Leslie to Bder Wells in the afternoon.	
" Jan 16th	Lt Campbell returned from leave to England. Went to No 4 F.A. in the afternoon — arr.	
" Jan 17th	Made arrangements about mending the road between HENU & Windmill near SOUASTRE, work for hedges, stone breakers, stones etc. arr.	
" Jan 18th	Lt Parfarlane proceeded on leave to England. Capt Mulhern takes over duties as M.O. & 9th Divn whilst he is on leave.	
" Jan 19th	Two Men & labour Battle. burnt to death in a billet during the night — Started road repairs — party of 40 men & N.C.O. employed from point 1520 m HENU Road to foot of west of mill outside SOUASTRE. Leave out the village. THE NUY 300 yds each side of it. arr.	

Army Form C. 2118.

WAR DIARY
or
INTELLIGENCE SUMMARY.

(Erase heading not required.)

Instructions regarding War Diaries and Intelligence Summaries are contained in F. S. Regs., Part II and the Staff Manual respectively. Title pages will be prepared in manuscript.

Hour, Date, Place	Summary of Events and Information	Remarks and references to Appendices
HENU Jan 20th	A & N.S 3) Hounier made an inspection in the morning. Went out to the advanced dressing station in the afternoon. Collected card with the evening.	Asylum By-Laws
" Jan 21st	Went down to S.A.S force H.Q.N.S in the afternoon. Out to advanced dressing station in the evening.	A.H.C.
" Jan 22nd	A & N.S 3) Hounier came up in the morning. Three P.H.S. Bristoe returned from temporary duty at both to Royal Munition.	A.H.C.
" Jan 23rd	Sunday. Church Parade in the morning. Campbell from out to H.Q.S the Bryan returned.	A.H.C.
" Jany 24th	Went out to advanced dressing station to the regimental aid post at Fond VILLERS.	R.H.C.

(73989) W4141—463. 400,000. 9/14. H.&J.Ltd. Forms/C. 2118/10.

Army Form C. 2118.

WAR DIARY
or
INTELLIGENCE SUMMARY.
(Erase heading not required.)

Instructions regarding War Diaries and Intelligence Summaries are contained in F. S. Regs., Part II. and the Staff Manual respectively. Title pages will be prepared in manuscript.

Hour, Date, Place	Summary of Events and Information	Remarks and references to Appendices
HENU July 25th	Walker Rowe proceeds to Gelvincourt on temporary a/c duty.	Marlyn Major Tower
" July 26th	A.D.M.S. 37 Division came round in the morning. Advanced HQrs. to PA's in the evening.	A.S.C.
" July 27th	Rendezvous in the "collecty" car in the morning to SOASTRE, ST AMAND, GAUDIAMPRE afterwards went to P.H.Q. of each for purpose paid the men in the afternoon. a supposed gas attack took place at FONQUIVILLERS at about 8pm	All
" July 28th	Heard officially that two promoted temp Lt Col in which in charge of 150 Field Ambulance as from July 11th 1915. Gazette dated 27th.	are
" July 29th	Major ___ has returned from leave during last month. Lt Harrison returned from temporary duty with R.M. R.O.S.A.C.	

WAR DIARY
or
INTELLIGENCE SUMMARY.
(Erase heading not required.)

Army Form C. 2118.

Hour, Date, Place	Summary of Events and Information	Remarks and references to Appendices
HENU Jany 30th	Sunday. Church Parade in the morning. Went out to Advanced dressing station in the evening	
" Jany 31st	At H.Q. 3/III Division came round the Field Ambulance in the morning. Advanced dressing station in the evening. A.H.	Asberlyn ibostrane

50th Field Ambulance

Feb 1916
March

50th F.A.
37th Div.
Vol. 3.

Feb 1916

Confidential

War Diary

of

Lieut Col. A. T. Carlyon R.A.M.C.
Commanding No. 50 Field Ambulance

From February 1 – 1916
To February 29. 1916

No. 50 Field Ambulance.

WAR DIARY
or
INTELLIGENCE SUMMARY.
(Erase heading not required.)

Army Form C. 2118.

Hour, Date, Place	Summary of Events and Information	Remarks and references to Appendices
HENU Feb 1/16	Shared the Divisional Rest Station. Lt Bousfield put in charge. Capt J. R. Cook R.A.M.C. arrived for duty.	
Feb 2nd	Being lay-out camp for our Rest Station. R.E. started putting up a couple of huts. Went out & advanced Mining Station in the evening.	
Feb 3rd	Capt Harrison Rowe left Institute 9th Leicesters. Reviewed path made Henderson to R.R.S. lines and down new line edge of path.	
Feb 4th	A.D.M.S. & 37 Division came up to inspect D.R.S. went out to advanced Mining Station in the evening.	
Feb 5th	Father Walsh 50.9.a r 4.8.2.a. advanced dressing Station in the evening.	
Feb 6th	Post Mortem performed in afternoon on body of a man found dead in the field – cause of death ruptured duodenal ulcer. Sapper McGovern 153 Field Co R.E. No. 104,751 R.E.	

No. 50 Field Ambulance

Army Form C. 2118.

WAR DIARY
or
INTELLIGENCE SUMMARY.
(Erase heading not required.)

Instructions regarding War Diaries and Intelligence Summaries are contained in F.S. Regs., Part II. and the Staff Manual respectively. Title pages will be prepared in manuscript.

Hour, Date, Place	Summary of Events and Information	Remarks and references to Appendices
# E N O Feb 7/15	A.D.M.S. came up from D.H.Q. in the morning. Letter received from Deputy Director Medical Services.	
Feb 8/15	A.D.M.S. came up in the morning. Started removing tables, chairs, bath, stove etc from the A.D.S. Went out there with Lieut. Campbell in the evening.	ADC
Feb 9/15	A.D.M.S. came up in the morning. Lt. Bryan goes on Trench duty as M.O. Willenwick.	AGL
Feb 10/15	Went down to P.A.S. Hotel Mons for personal hair cut in the afternoon. Lt. J. McColahan proceeded on leave to England.	ADC
Feb 11/15	Hubat & R.S. completed receipt for the stores. Went out to A.D.S. in evening though I took down more table etc.	ADC

No. 50 Field Ambulance

Army Form C. 2118.

WAR DIARY
or
INTELLIGENCE SUMMARY.
(Erase heading not required.)

Hour, Date, Place	Summary of Events and Information	Remarks and references to Appendices
HQ NW Zillebeke	D.A.D.M.S came up in the afternoon & stayed the night. Went out to A.D.S in the evening.	
Feb 13th	Major Laine goes on leave duty to U.K. Bedford in place of Capt Gillespie RAMC. Advanced Dressing Station at Fosse VIII R.S. Given up from to day. Capt Waythorn DADMS Completed take over duties of medical officers of Battalions returned. A.D.M.S came up in the morning.	
Feb 14th	S.D.M.S 37 Division admitted to Field Ambulance. Checked all equipment returned from A.D.S. etc.	
Feb 15th	DADMS evacuated to C.C.S. Captains Rouse & Ingoldby join the 13th Royal Fusiliers. Capt Halberg goes to relieve Capt Bryan who returns to day.	
Feb 16th	Lt Hindler arrived for duty being relieved by Capt Cook. Gale of wind, numbers blown down - floods & rain. a D.M.S 37 Division came up from PHC in the evening. AGC	

No. 50 Field Ambulance

Army Form C. 2118.

WAR DIARY
or
INTELLIGENCE SUMMARY.
(Erase heading not required.)

Instructions regarding War Diaries and Intelligence Summaries are contained in F.S. Regs., Part II. and the Staff Manual respectively. Title pages will be prepared in manuscript.

Hour, Date, Place	Summary of Events and Information	Remarks and references to Appendices
HENU Feb 7th	Sale Journal four tentloom down - arrangements made to take over Divisional baths at 9AS on departure of 149 Field Ambulance — Approx of motor ambulances by C.O. R.A.W. collection of stretcher	
Feb 8th	46 Bryan proceed on leave today à Sml 37 Division Ambce. came here this morning are	
Feb 19th	Moved down to PAS in the afternoon & took over the S are	
" Feb 20th	Sgt W Colahan returned from leave. O/walks returned from temporary duty are	
" Feb 21st	Divisional H.Q. removed from PAS to BAVINCOURT. Inspected Divisional baths at PAS. Lts Marshall Raine are in charge	
" Feb 22nd	Heavy fall of Snow - arrived 2 more wood for floors AH. of huts C.R.S.	

No. 50 Field Ambulance

WAR DIARY
or
INTELLIGENCE SUMMARY
(Erase heading not required.)

Army Form C. 2118.

Hour, Date, Place	Summary of Events and Information	Remarks and references to Appendices
HE No Feb 23rd	Went in the betting car to MARLINCOURT to collect kit & valise went to GHQ to inspect the div. baths & OMS came round in the afternoon etc.	
" Feb 24th	Went to BAVINCOURT to see a GMS draw mops for personnel. Walked on to BAVIMPRÉ as M.O. of down battn (temp) – now want to no coy RFA (temp) det our battn (temp) – now want to no coy RFA (temp) ARC	
" Feb 25th	Severe blizzard. Detailed to proceed to HAVRE ARC.	
" Feb 26th	Snowstorm all day – my kit & gear (my luggage) was in pieces a T.M. came round – ARC.	
" Feb 27th	Sunday – Walker returned from eight days duty at BAVIMPRÉ	
" Feb 28th	M⁰ Ferguson Anderson arrived for duty from the Base. Are S. Walker leaves for permanent duty on no 1/c + 59th F Ambs. are	
" Feb 29th	Several our patients transferred from no 9 F.A. & R. Ryan returned from leave.	

A.H.Esson
Lt Col RAMC

Confidential

War Diary

of

Lieut. Col. A. F. Carlyon R.A.M.C.
O.C. 50 Field Ambulance

From 1 March 1916   To 31 March 1916

50 Field Ambulance

WAR DIARY
or
INTELLIGENCE SUMMARY.
(Erase heading not required.)

Army Form C. 2118.

Instructions regarding War Diaries and Intelligence Summaries are contained in F.S. Regs., Part II. and the Staff Manual respectively. Title pages will be prepared in manuscript.

Hour, Date, Place	Summary of Events and Information	Remarks and references to Appendices
HENU March 1st	Inspection by A.D.M.S. in the morning, went out to TONGVILLERS afterward, saw the C.A.S.V/3rd Division F.A. about looking after cases belonging to the division. Made arrangements with them about horse care brought H.Q. of the F.A. a spade where they will be fetched by us — Arthur Holland	
March 2nd	A dead foot hospl in (Pte Blaire 11 Royal Scots Fusiliers) run over by motor lorry in F.A.S. reaction of pupils hopeless. 130 men of 49 F.A. billeted in a hut belonging to R.S. A.H.	
March 3rd	A S.M.S. visited us in the morning. Severe blizzard.	
March 4th	Blizzard. Horses from 49 F.A. brought around to our stables for shelter.	
March 5th	A.D.M.S. 7th Corps inspected the Field Ambulance. A.H.	
March 6th	Blizzard. All work except that about the Reservoir suspended. Inclemency of the weather A.H.	
March 7th	Inspection of Divisional Baths & Gas saw S.M.S. & their dental surgeon from Souleu came to see patients. V.For Farlane returned from temporary duty A.H.	

50 Field Ambulance

WAR DIARY or INTELLIGENCE SUMMARY.

Army Form C. 2118.

Hour, Date, Place	Summary of Events and Information	Remarks and references to Appendices
HENU March 8th	Conference at BAVINCOURT at A.D.M.S. Office Saturday afternoon	
" March 9th	Fire alarm 7 a.m. - chimney on fire - put out with difficulty. Lecture to orderlies started by D.M.O.	
" March 10th	A.D.M.S came up in the afternoon. A/Lce Cpl 4457 a Personnel left today for Battalions except 21 officers & men for Field Amb. Snow Storm. Lecture to orderlies by D.M.O. A.M.	
" March 11th	A Staff Officer from 4th Division came to see the Chateau with a view of its being taken over as divisional H.Q. for 4th Div.	
" March 12th	Inspection 2 smoke helmets. Paid the personnel. Church parade. a D.M.S 4th Division came to look at new A.D.S. the Chateau	
" March 13th	Conference at A.D.M.S. Office BAVINCOURT. O.C. No 117a came to see chateau (he will take it over from us)	

WAR DIARY or INTELLIGENCE SUMMARY.

Army Form C. 2118.

50 Field Ambulance

Instructions regarding War Diaries and Intelligence Summaries are contained in F. S. Regs., Part II and the Staff Manual respectively. Title pages will be prepared in manuscript.

(Erase heading not required.)

Hour, Date, Place	Summary of Events and Information	Remarks and references to Appendices
HÉNU March 14th	Went to HAUTVISEE to arrange into accommodation for the Field Ambulance with 2nd Colahan (2 i/c) or Strand, we were for 12 more there — Orders received to proceed, transport move received in the evening.	April weather
" March 15th	All F.S. wagons loaded & sent off to HAUTVISEE to dig with first load of equipment. A & M.S. & S.T. & DON's 4 Division came to see that our of are	
" March 16th	A & M.S. 37 Division + 2 V.O. & Offs in came round. Another load of equipment sent to HAUTVISEE. Flame Projector demonstration at LA CAUCHÉE	are
" March 17th	Advanced park (20 men + 1 N.C.O.) went on to HAUTVISEE	are
" March 18th	Left HÉNU for HAUTVISEE at 9 a.m. arrived there at 3 p.m. — 50 men cut their billets & found billets for officers — patients put into the farm —	are

Army Form C. 2118.

50 Field Ambulance
WAR DIARY
or
INTELLIGENCE SUMMARY.
(Erase heading not required.)

Instructions regarding War Diaries and Intelligence Summaries are contained in F. S. Regs., Part II and the Staff Manual respectively. Title pages will be prepared in manuscript.

Hour, Date, Place	Summary of Events and Information	Remarks and references to Appendices
HAUT VISÉE March 19	Went out in the Motor Car to explore the new collecting area - busy unpacking resorting equipment	ARE StothAME
" March 20th	Two Staff Officers came round in the morning. General Commander came round in the afternoon. Squad drill 6.30-7.15 - Route march 9-11.30. Lectures 2-4	ARE
" March 21st	A.D.M.S. 37 Division made an inspection. Revd Nick Wesleyan Minister arrived to be attached to the Units. Squad drill 6.30-7.15 Route march 9-11.30	ARE
" March 22nd	Went to LUCHEUX tree a 8pm. Inspection of Billets, men's cookhouse etc. Squad drill 6.30-7.15 Lectures 2-4	ARE
" March 23rd	Squad drill 6.30-7.15. Stretcher work 8-10am	ARE
" March 24th	Near fall of snow. Lectures to orderlies 2-4 pm	ARE

WAR DIARY or INTELLIGENCE SUMMARY.

Army Form C. 2118.

5'O Field Ambulance

(Erase heading not required.)

Hour, Date, Place	Summary of Events and Information	Remarks and references to Appendices
HAUT VISEE March 25th	S/Sgt M.S. 37th Division R.A.M.C. Instructor from O.C. before came to show the personnel how to put on their Marching Order Kit. Squad drill 6.30 - 7.15am. Stretcher work 2-4pm. A. Marshall Major	
March 26th	Sunday. 1 W.O. & 9 men detailed for permanent duty at Frevent South Sub Factory DOULLENS. A.H. Church Parade 11.20am.	
March 27th	Squad drill 6.30 - 7.15am. Route march 9-11.30am Lecture 2-4pm 4 patients transferred from 4th Divisional Rest Station H.E.M.Y. Capt.	
March 28th	Squad drill 6.30 - 7.15am. Stretcher work 2-4pm 2 O.R.S. 37th Division came round in the afternoon A.H.C	
March 29th	Squad drill 6.30 - 7.15am. Divisional Baths 3.30 - 3pm (T.A.S) went into town to make arrangement about divisional cases. A.H.C	
March 30th	Squad drill 6.30 - 7.15am. Stretcher work 8-10pm Inspection by A.D.M.S 37th Division A.H.C	
March 31st	Squad drill 6.30 - 7.15am. Afternoon spent in digging trench 6 feet deep for stretcher exercises A.H.C	

April 1916

War Diary

of

Lieut Col A. F. Caryon R.A.M.C

Commanding No 50 Field Ambulance

From 1st April 1916 To 30th April 1916

50 Field Ambulance

WAR DIARY
or
INTELLIGENCE SUMMARY.
(Erase heading not required.)

Army Form C. 2118.

Instructions regarding War Diaries and Intelligence Summaries are contained in F. S. Regs., Part II and the Staff Manual respectively. Title pages will be prepared in manuscript.

Hour, Date, Place	Summary of Events and Information	Remarks and references to Appendices
HAUT VISEÉ April 1st	Route march 2 - 4:30pm -	Appell blosure are.
" April 2nd	Sunday - Church parade 11 am — Route march 2 - 4:30pm -	are.
" April 3rd	Lt ELLIOTT R.A.M.C. transferred to No: 48 Field Amb'ce to duty. Squad drill 6:30 – 7:15 am – Trench stretcher work	are
April 4th	Route march 2 - 5pm.	are
April 5th	Route march — Column Parade by Section, inspection by W.O.'s N.C.O's & men in rain.	are
April 6th	Trench stretcher work 2 - 4:30pm	are
April 7th	Genl Joffre passed through the village, personnel formed up lined the street. Lieut Fletcher gave over Squad drill 6:30 – 7:15 am. Route march 2 - 4:30 pm	A.Y.C.
" April 9th	Squad drill 6:30 – 7:15 am. Trench stretcher work 9 - 11:30	A.Y.C.

Army Form C. 2118.

WAR DIARY
or
INTELLIGENCE SUMMARY.
(Erase heading not required.)

50 Field Ambulance

Instructions regarding War Diaries and Intelligence Summaries are contained in F.S. Regs., Part II. and the Staff Manual respectively. Title pages will be prepared in manuscript.

Hour, Date, Place	Summary of Events and Information	Remarks and references to Appendices

HACIT VIS E/E April 1915. Sunday. Church parade 11am. Working parties in Ravine.

" April 11th Started repairing the walls of the billets. Have projected demonstrational BATH. Inspection at Arms Office 2.30 pm — AJC

" April 11th Bryan foreman temp duty in M.O. 1/c 6th Bedfords whilst Capt Hunter Powis is on leave. AJC

" April 13th Lt Ferguson goes on leave to Ireland. Route march (what to postponed on account of weather) Personnel paid in the afternoon. AJC

" April 13th too inclement weather. Lecture on First aid to cases. AJC

" April 14th All leave stopped - telegrams sent to those on leave instructing them to two channel not later than 18th. Inoculation with T.A.B. serum twice out AJC

WAR DIARY or INTELLIGENCE SUMMARY

Army Form C. 2118.

50 Field Ambulance

Hour, Date, Place	Summary of Events and Information	Remarks and references to Appendices
HQ UT VISE April 15th	Two new Officers arrived for duty Capt MAWHOLE HARKIN (both temp) 6.30-7.15am squad drill. 9-11.30 trench stretcher work. 31 men inoculated with T.A.B. serum Artillery fire heavy	
April 16th	Sunday. Church parade 11am	
April 17th	A.O.M.S. came & inspected us 33 men inoculated with T.A.B. 6.30-7.15am squad drill. 9-11.30 loading & unloading wagons 2-4 pm lectures.	
April 18th	Practised preparing advanced dressing stations & moving patients from trenches into them	
April 19th	D.M.S. 3rd Army made an inspection of the field Ambulance. Continued advanced dressing in practice. 23 men inoculated with T.A.B.	
April 20th	Lt Ferguson RAMC returned from leave Squad drill 6.30-7.15am. Route March 10-12. Lectures in the afternoon. 8 men inoculated with T.A.B.	

WAR DIARY
or
INTELLIGENCE SUMMARY.

Army Form C. 2118.

(Erase heading not required.)

50 Field Ambulance

Instructions regarding War Diaries and Intelligence Summaries are contained in F.S. Regs., Part II. and the Staff Manual respectively. Title pages will be prepared in manuscript.

Hour, Date, Place	Summary of Events and Information	Remarks and references to Appendices
HAUTVISEE April 21st	Visit from ADMS 37th Division. Practice in preparation for A.D.S. Practice inoculated with T.A.B. 7 men inoculated with T.A.B.	A Marlyn Lt Colonel
" April 22nd	Squad drill 6.30–7.15 am. Route march 11–12–20. Went to Doullens to inspect the billets the men from SDA employed on fatigues at the food station. 7 men inoculated with T.A.B.	AM
" April 23rd	Church Parade 11 am. Conference LtHE UX at 2pm at ADMS Office. 11 men inoculated with T.A.B.	AM
" April 24th	Visit from ADMS in the morning. Practice in preparation for ADS trench stretcher work. 5 men inoculated with T.A.B.	AM
" April 25th	Squad drill 6.30–7.15 am. Route march 10.30–12.30. Lectures in afternoon. 9 men inoculated with T.A.B.	AM
" April 26th	Conference at ADMS Office at 11.30 am. Inspected the land in the valley D RNS ART with a view to the manoeuvre to be held there next week. 2 men inoculated with T.A.B.	AM

50 Field Ambulance

WAR DIARY
or
INTELLIGENCE SUMMARY.

Army Form C. 2118.

Hour, Date, Place	Summary of Events and Information	Remarks and references to Appendices
HAUT VISÉE April 27th	Children's fête at Luchieure in afternoon. Squad drill 6.30–7.15 am. Route March 10.30–12.30. 7 men mounted with TMB arrangements.	
" April 28th	A & B go on leave. Stores over to duties. Went to Luchieure to unite makers with him. He left in the afternoon, being beginning tomorrow. 5 men mounted with TMB	ALC
" April 29th	Sudden orders received for the Division to move from Div. Rest into the line. Chose three places for the A.D.S. to be viz. LA HERLIÈRE, STAMAND, MENU but when returned to Luchieure was told by A.Q.M.G.S. that the two latter places could not be taken permanently but that STAMAND might be used as a temporary measure. 3 men mounted with TMB	ALC
" April 30th	Saw D.D.M.S. 7th Corps at Pas. It was decided to send SD7a to LA HERLIÈRE + have two ADS.'s for the F.a. at BERLES + BAIDLEVAL respectively = 4972 + 4879 to STAMAND with an ADS at HENU-BLENVILLERS? to HUMBERCAMP which look will on peace as temp measure.	ALC

37th Divs
50 F. Amb
Vol 8

Confidential

May 19th

War Diary

of

Lieut. Col. A. T. Carlyon R.A.M.C.
O.C. 50 Field Ambulance

From MAY 1st 1916   To MAY 31st 1916

COMMITTEE FOR THE
MEDICAL HISTORY OF THE WAR
Date   26 JUN 1915

5D Field Ambulance

WAR DIARY or INTELLIGENCE SUMMARY

Army Form C. 2118.

Hour, Date, Place	Summary of Events and Information	Remarks and references to Appendices
HAUTVISÉE May 1st	Capt Way goes on leave - 2 Cholera for a lump duty - Went to conference at SITOL with a MOs. The other division F.A.s army - found a suitable place for Nos 4 & 7 F.A. tomorrow from HUMBER CAMP at COUTURELLE - No 5D F.A move tomorrow to LAHERLIÈRE -	amartin 2tb Raine
LAHERLIÈRE May 2nd	Moved SD F.A. to LAHERLIÈRE where we from No 10 F.A. to F meeting reach at the 40's for reception behinds. A.D.S's situated at BERLES & BAVINCVAL. A/K	
— May 3rd	No 4 & 87 F.A. moved from LUCHEUX to HUMBER CAMP. Saw DDMS & Col. f.s. met HDMS & 46 Div: at PAS showed him round the divisional baths there. Lt Cockerane arrived fairly No 4 & 7 F.A. move from MONDICOURT to SLAYMAND	
" May 4th	Severe fighting during the night. 4.5 wounded admitted to No SD F.A. evacuated to CCS during the morning. also 1 officer. All from A.D.S at BERLE. went through to both ADSs in the afternoon. A/K	

(73989) W4141—463. 400,000. 9/14. H.&J., Ltd. Forms/C. 2118/10.

50 Field Ambulance

WAR DIARY
or
INTELLIGENCE SUMMARY.

Army Form C. 2118.

Hour, Date, Place	Summary of Events and Information	Remarks and references to Appendices
LA HERIÉRE May 5th	Lt HARKIN goes for duty with 9th Leicesters. Went out to both advanced dressing stations. Weather warm	
" May 6th	497.a moves from STANKAND to LABRET to 87.a moves from HUMBERCAMP to COOTUREUS. Went to both these places in the afternoon & found them ready for reception of patients.	A.g.L.
" May 7th	A.D.M.S. returned from leave – went to his office in the afternoon – went out to both A.D.S's in the evening.	A.g.L
" May 9th	Capt Paterson goes on leave. Lt Bolam sent to duty with 9th Leicesters in place of Lt Harkin who returned to 50 F.A. Went to see A.D.M.S in the afternoon & to his A.D.S. = in the Evening	A.r.C.
" May 9th	Usual hospital routine – a very wet day	A.r.C.
" May 10th	A.D.M.S came to inspect Field Ambulance. Paid the Personnel in the afternoon –	A.r.C.

50 Field Ambulance

WAR DIARY
or
INTELLIGENCE SUMMARY.

Army Form C. 2118.

Hour, Date, Place	Summary of Events and Information	Remarks and references to Appendices
LA HERLIÈRE May 11th	Capt Way returned from leave. Went out to both A.D.S's in the afternoon. Decided to take over the shelter in each place leaving 10 men at our own - Also made up the strength of personnel to 20 at each place. 10 patients.	
" May 12th	Went out to the A.D.S's in the evening. In the afternoon Capt War self went out to examine the surrounding country in regards roads etc. A.M.	
May 13th	Very inclement weather - had to keep entirely A.T.L.	
May 14th	Church Parade 11 a.m.	
May 15th	Board on Remount Race Horse in the afternoon. A.D.M.S 27th Division President.	A.T.C.
May 16th	Went out to both A.D.S. — in the afternoon.	are
May 17th	Inspection of Field Ambulance by the Divisional Commander 10 a.m.	A.T.L.
May 18th	Capt Paterson returned from leave - handed over duties to him & started on leave.	A.T.L.

50 Field Ambulance —

WAR DIARY
or
INTELLIGENCE SUMMARY.

(Erase heading not required.)

Army Form C. 2118.

Hour, Date, Place	Summary of Events and Information	Remarks and references to Appendices
LA HERLIERE May 28	Returned from leave at Issoire. Went out to troops advanced dressing station in the afternoon. A/Major McGann	
" May 29	A D Ms & 37 Division came round. Major on return from NCOs at BAILLEUVAL relieved by Lt Bryson. — Capt Macleisters from BERLES to be relieved by Lt Macleister — 10 men relieved from each A.D.S. by new men. A.H.C.	
" May 30/18	Returned for poisoning treatment by Lt Graham 11.23 pm a/nos=49 F a. Lunched with A.D.S. in evening. E. A.H.	
" May 31/18	Went out to the advanced dressing station in the evening. A.H.C.	

Confidential

From
   Officer Commanding
     50 Field Ambulance

To O/c
    A.G.'s Office
      Base.

Herewith War Diary of this Unit for the month of June 1916 please.

                                    Capt. R.A.M.C.,
                         Commanding 50th Field Ambulance.

1/7/16

Stamp: 50TH FIELD AMBULANCE — 1 JUL 1916

50 Field Amb
Vol 9
June

Confidential
June 16

War Diary

of

Lieut Col A. F. Carlyon R.A.M.C. Officer Commanding
No 50 Field Ambulance up to 29th June 1916.

and

Capt M. W. Paterson R.A.M.C. Officer Commanding No 50 Field
Ambulance from that date.

From June 1- 1916
To June 30- 1916

COMMITTEE FOR THE
MEDICAL HISTORY OF THE WAR
Date 5 AUG. 1916

50 Field Ambulance

WAR DIARY
INTELLIGENCE SUMMARY.

Army Form C. 2118.

Hour, Date, Place	Summary of Events and Information	Remarks and references to Appendices
LA HERLIERE June 1st	Went out to A.D.S. at BERLES. Made arrangements with Town Major about taking over a cellar in a village of accommodation of wounded showed Nurse-Lt Arie Mcaffing there	A.Halpin Lt/Col
" June 2nd	Went out to A.D.S. at BAILLEUVAL inspected the F.A. A.P.s. well as A.D.S.	A.H.
" June 3rd	Capt Shaw sent out to the 8 F.A. Stopford took over medical charge 89th Bgde. Lt Whitmore R.A.M.C. arrived for duty. A.D.M.S. 3rd Division came to visit in the afternoon	A.H.
" June 4th	Twelve wounded from Berles during the night 20 mg Crew round with morning church parade 11 a.m.	A.H.
" June 5th	Went out to both A.D.S. in the afternoon - Much excitement caused by the fact a Thunderstorm Burst but fortunately took but no damage done	A.H.

50 Field Ambulance

WAR DIARY or INTELLIGENCE SUMMARY

Army Form C. 2118.

Hour, Date, Place	Summary of Events and Information	Remarks and references to Appendices
LA HERLIE RE June 6th	Went to 152 Co. RE to try to get pipes & lamps for a superior bath. Went on to both A.D.S. in the evening. A.M.C.	specially for entrance
" June 7th	Heard of the death of Lord Kitchener. A gramophone presented by Revd Miller S.C.F. A.M.C.	
" June 8th	Lt Whitmore sent to Art.S at Berles in place of Lt Harkin who returned here for duty. A.M.C.	
" June 9th	S.M.5. 3rd Worc went to make an inspection, each Section sent 1/f R.C. orderlies to render all skin "exceptff etc. In the picture - and the men to practice stretcher drill. A.M.C.	
" June 10th	A.D.S. Souez a bombardment of La BRET dressing station was begun, lasted until about 9 a.m. 120 shells being fired, about the first 20 shells or so fell in the village, three houses in the field ambulance were wounded as also one of the personnel all being sent to C.C.S. Horses turn out & stampeded, three mules and 6 being recovered. Two horses were wounded & evacuated. A.M.C.	

50 Field Ambulance

WAR DIARY
or
INTELLIGENCE SUMMARY.
(Erase heading not required.)

Army Form C. 2118.

Instructions regarding War Diaries and Intelligence Summaries are contained in F. S. Regs., Part II. and the Staff Manual respectively. Title pages will be prepared in manuscript.

Hour, Date, Place	Summary of Events and Information	Remarks and references to Appendices
LA HERLIERE June 11th	Conference at A.D.M.S. Office "Evacuation of wounded during severe fighting" Church parade 6 p.m. Angry gun continue	
June 12th	Went out to 9th A.D.S. in the afternoon. A.D.M.S. 3rd Division came round in the evening. A.H.	
June 13th	Memorial Service to Lord Kitchener in the morning at LA CAUCHE. 2 Officers, 1 N.C.O. & 12 men attended. A.H.	

Army Form C. 2118.

WAR DIARY
or
INTELLIGENCE SUMMARY.
(Erase heading not required.)

Instructions regarding War Diaries and Intelligence Summaries are contained in F. S. Regs., Part II. and the Staff Manual respectively. Title pages will be prepared in manuscript.

Hour, Date, Place	Summary of Events and Information	Remarks and references to Appendices
June 27th.	Lieut Col. Carlyon having gone Sick and sicknow to Hosp. O.C.S. his place being taken by Capt A. Patterson. Then 2nd in Command of the Unit, who was invalided from the Advanced Dressing Station at Berles. MDP. Col. Swan visited the Ambulance with Brig. Gen. R.J. Pritney D.A.D.M.S. VII Corps. Capt. Clowes T.O. reported for duty at Unit H.Q. Heavy firing during night. MDP	
June 28th	A.D.M.S. visited the Unit. Prisoners, 1a Bavarian, Hindenburgh stated by enemy, 2 men & 1 officer surrendered result they were taken at 1.30 pm C/S, by us, all wearing steamed respirators. Capt Nicholson 10th L N Lancs having died from wounds Res Major & Rev J.R. Scott R.C.P.C. Captain. Shortly in evening as casualties were expected MDP Positions not known. 670 wounded cases evacuated 17th May. Successful raids on enemy trenches MDP	
June 29th	Night passed with out incident. A.D.M.S. visited Unit W. M.T. Convoys ever Unit. Visited Ballerine & Bertles. Advanced Dressing Stations with Capt Clowes. MDP A.D.M.S. visited Unit at 7-15 am Very few admissions during day.	

A.D. Patterson Capt R.A.M.C.

Confidential
July 1/16

50 Field Amb
Vol 10
July

War Diary
of
M. W. Paterson
Capt R.A.M.C
O.C. 50 Field Ambulance

From July 1916   To 31 July 1916

(Volume 10)

COMMITTEE FOR THE
MEDICAL HISTORY OF THE WAR
Date 5 SEP 16

WAR DIARY or INTELLIGENCE SUMMARY

Army Form C. 2118

O.C. 60th Field Amb.

Place	Date	Hour	Summary of Events and Information	Remarks and references to Appendices
Laterlière	1 7/16		A.D.M.S. visited the Ambulance in the morning. Capt. Clows & Self visited Bailleulval & A.D.S. in the afternoon & proceeded to the Bsoli* A.D.S. By Sunken Rd & Field Ambulance Advanced Post No 2. Found A.D.M.S. at Bsoli. J.W.P.	⊕ map 57C 1:40,000 W.4.9.3.9. ∗ ditto W.15.C.6.3.
"	2 7/16		Col. Simm D.D.M.S. 7th Corps visited Ambulance & stated probability of more Battle having died down after the Gommecourt fight, very few casualties occurred. Relieved Revd Bryan at A.D.S. Revd Whitam taking his place. Also shortened at Berles by Capt. Dillon. J.W.P.	
"	3 7/16		Received intimation to present Mondicourt F.A. Station from 2/3 London F. Amb. Here. Found on arrival of line the last that C.O. knew nothing of this + that no one should have A.D.M.S. who explained that a suitable Post had been arranged with Col. of Lettres Pacts 8 & 9. Written & Capt. in afternoon passage both to C.O. & Lettres Laterlière from us. Received ambulance & fraction to proceed & Laudrincourt & to morning. Reserve estimation carried out. Capt Long presentment a present was on. J.W.P.	
Laudrincourt	4 7/16		Moved party. Arrived at 5. and 4 & 8 R stretcher also coming in to same village. Sound Billets & front intry. Cap. 462 Filant Lorthier hospital, 50 & Lane Fever. Attended to them & closed down. Raised for the present. Kadgs with frontbrands continued. Finish. J.W.P.	
"	5 7/16		Ordered out equipment. Returns kinship altgether. G.R.O. Art. p.42 from hosp. letters Mondicourt. Also returned all extra medical stores & armour and photos stove. Laterlière & Surplus Red & S.R.&S.U Trench at them. Engine parked & surplus more Within an hour. A.D.M.S. visited ambulance in morning. J.W.P.	

WAR DIARY
or
INTELLIGENCE SUMMARY
(Erase heading not required.)

Army Form C. 2118

Instructions regarding War Diaries and Intelligence Summaries are contained in F. S. Regs., Part II. and the Staff Manual respectively. Title Pages will be prepared in manuscript.

Place	Date	Hour	Summary of Events and Information	Remarks and references to Appendices
Sautricourt	July 6th Thursday		Division split up by bodies of Infantry Brigades to other Divisions. 2 horsed Ambulances & 60 & 61 F. Amb. following troops in new area. Detailed remaining horsed amb with 3 officers 46 & 70 F. Amb, of which Amb: Spellow-Roselli Brigade. Passed through Rev. at 2 p.m. After Battle for Germans count road Backwards to Artillery bombardments, very few wounded coming in at all. Heavy rain late afternoon, & all night.	JWP
"	July 7th		Training started. Troops R. in. Employed to fit. 70 so F. Amb; undertook sanitation of hospital area, & village fatigues of train Cadre. Very hot day. Had no route march in morning.	JWP
"	July 8th		A.D.M.S. visited unit at 9-20. With Capt: Clavers visited Grunnoe, & the big sized place for resting & showing station. No place suitable found. (Aix paid) scratch day in afternoon	JWP
"	July 9th		Church parade with 46 F. Amb. Rode over to 20 C.C.S. at Lumbrescourt & talk in afternoon. In evening walked out of Somewhere - Congratters R, of watch bombardment, which was nothin sensational. Saw few wrecked German lines, probably Some village, Everywhere signs up of activity. Received Army order of the Day, stating H.A.'s congratulations to troops on the offensive.	JWP
"	July 10th		The unit went for a days route march at 9-30 taking fast Breaks & returned at 5 p.m.	JWP
"	July 11th July 12th		In morning the officers tested the men of the unit on first aid. In afternoon the N.C.Os conducted a practical class in nursing, bandaging etc.	JWP
"	July 13th		As the village is in such a deplorable state, felt the S.M. of the unit were placed at the disposal of the Town Major, for help & tidy up drainages R., commenced Divisional Baths & Repair the roads.	JWP
*Houdain- Heurignauel	July 14th		Orders for moving forth came from A.D.M.S. in morning. A.D.M.S. visits Ambulance at 10-30 *Graph src. Capt: Gillen & Pt. Q-R. Callahan (Refirst) 1-20 with advanced Party. Pt: Backer Lionaine with 10,000 ft. 14 A. 2 Amb cars & 3 horsed Ambs, & follow. 103 Bde, Marching 4 Guns, Tanks etc., or ourselves in evening. Ambs Revel out at 2-0 p.m. Pmeinke, via Conturille - Soubrin - Grand Rullecourt- Hervin.	JWP

1875 Wt. W593/826 1,000,000 4/15 J.B.C. & A. A.D.S.S./Forms/C. 2118.

Army Form C. 2118.

WAR DIARY
or
INTELLIGENCE SUMMARY.
(Erase heading not required.)

Instructions regarding War Diaries and Intelligence Summaries are contained in F. S. Regs., Part II. and the Staff Manual respectively. Title pages will be prepared in manuscript.

Place	Date	Hour	Summary of Events and Information	Remarks and references to Appendices
Mesnil – Hennencourt	July 14th/15th	3:30 pm	Arrived Henvin 7 – 3:30 pm. & find Capt. Dillon had arranged billets for all. The 34th of Fd Ambs & 164 F.S.Co in Sam's village. The 103rd Brigade arrived during night 14 – 15th along with Ambulances in charge of Staff Baker. Walker fine early.	Infp. ⊕ 36.B. T.17.C.
Sharpnay	15th		Resumed first duties at 9.30 am. following 103rd Bgds. Two Regiments – Gony – Fizy St Michel – Hargney arrived 3 pm. The Ambs Advanced party as yesterday carrying in sick evacuated from — 56 stragglers many elderly, few were collected in the march by horse Ambulances & Machinery lorries. Ambs fell out 12 returned to their units during the day. Drive A.D.M.S. at Hergneswil in evening.	1/10,000 T.17.C. Jw.W.P.
"	16th (Sun)		Kit inspection – Foot inspection – Church parade 10.30 am. Several troops passed through the village in the afternoon, for Bray 113rd Bgds (Aynscombe's Brd) & 157 Co R.E. billeted in the village.	Jw.W.P.
"	17th		Being Inspn. A.D.M.S. visits the Tank. transfers the temporary hospital & horse lines. Rest with Capt. Boyd at St-Pol in afternoon.	Jw.W.P.
"	18th		Showery day – cleaning tabs. Lt/Capt Dillon visits probably Rewards of Division. Tracklies to Hernin, as A.D.M.S. had intended to take the tabs Earl of Mort. Asst A.D.M.S. to Hernin also informed As at abstraction to movement, rested on line Bray & Hernin. States are no ordering. Informed 103 Bgds operation.	Jw.W.P.
Bray	19th		M4 sent to bed off in Ford early at 9 – 30 am. Having Ambulances in charge of Scout Baker. Artillerie Brigade. Advance rapidly with Capt. Dillon + H.Qm. Oblohan procured 7 gun truck followed. – Froncy – Bruton – hagnicourt – Herwelin – la Comte – Houdain – Division. Bray. Arrived 4-30 pm & in prepared billets for the Clearing stn.– hospital. Confirmed 2 vacant. – Hernich billets hurried adequate about 120 Hosp. all sittings in the Courtyard had been chipped by the Sergeants in the neighbourhood. Lieut Baker & turnip at 6 pm.	Infp. ⊕ 36.B. 1/40,000 J.21.G. Jw.W.P.

WAR DIARY
or
~~INTELLIGENCE SUMMARY~~

(Erase heading not required.)

Army Form C. 2118.

Instructions regarding War Diaries and Intelligence Summaries are contained in F. S. Regs., Part II. and the Staff Manual respectively. Title pages will be prepared in manuscript.

Place	Date	Hour	Summary of Events and Information	Remarks and references to Appendices
Bruay	July 20th		Parade 9-30. The men were told of their Special care not to cause any offence to the inhabitants. Physical Drill 10 a.m. The day was spent joining new billets etc.	
" "	21st		Letter from Asst D.G. from a Divisional Rest Station. Wrote same line. The hospital cooks were replied upon. Visited 20.22.C.C.S. Major Cloydwin in Charge. All NCO's & Men. Hts on parade at 6-5.5 a.m. Stopping Massy. This order was issued as some slackness was observed. Sent all Officers and details for duty with the Divisional Supply column.	
" "	22nd		Light work morning. All Men on fatigue. Route March in afternoon. Capt Loy & I visited Hosp. & Rest. Camp Personnel. Lieut Bryson 480 Lon Regt. for Bois de Dieppe, Sean Heythuysen, to carry out See Allory & Fatigue Duties there.	
" "	23rd		A.D.M.S. visits the Ambulance in Morning. Hosp A & G Book Closed, only S.R.S. and Books kept open. Church Parade 10-30 a.m. Pte Whitham Reliefs from Supply Train. Pries Pte Russell, who reported for duty at 6 p.m.	
" "	24th		The Divi Supply Column having to retreat Officers. The Asst Dent had Officers in Charge of the T.P.O. was & Faithell. Wire morning, Sick Daily. Recives instructions from A.D.M.S & visit of the London F. Amb. at Estree Cauchie & outlying posts (which attached with view to taking over from this Amb. Presents in afternoon with Capt Mays & Soldier of Cauconit. D.A.D.M.S. Lt Colonel paid Amb a visit.	⊕ App 51.C. F.J.3.S.
" "	25th		Detailed Lt Robson + left Sercus + Privers with 23 men of Mint of Cathie White over Advanced Dressing Station there. Detailed Lt Mackenzie & 3 Drivers at Cauconet work for Dr Parsons a complete equipment for Dr Seddon, & rates. Over Divisional Rest Station there. Col. Hard. R.C.A.M.C. of L.D.S. of 6 Cufs. Grnits the Ambulances at 10.30 a.m. with Lt Col Colahan. I visited Head quarters of the 4th London VAD Ambulance & made final arrangements for taking over to-morrow.	* App 36.B. V 5.E. U. E.

WAR DIARY
or
INTELLIGENCE SUMMARY

Army Form C. 2118.

(Erase heading not required.)

Instructions regarding War Diaries and Intelligence Summaries are contained in F. S. Regs., Part II. and the Staff Manual respectively. Title pages will be prepared in manuscript.

Place	Date	Hour	Summary of Events and Information	Remarks and references to Appendices
Etrits-Anchie	July 26th	9-0 a.m.	Capt. Dillon & advanced party left Bray at 9-0 a.m. The Ambulance proceeded in two parties, ① under Capt: Clowes with 2 horsed Ambulances, birth stretcher – Major Bruce & stretcher party for the camp, as our other unit took over from this Brancroft a small party of mounted – 2nd dealing was left (Ecantain.) to relieve this camp until arrival of the Town Major's men took charge. The Ambulance moved out at 7-30 prompt via Hentain – Rocles court – Bouchu – Syd – Estrees-Anchie, arrived 12-30. Col: Jamin O.O. 1/5 London F. Amb. moved offices 2 p.m. & finally left a party to clean up depot this unit took over. It is worthy of note that this is the cleanest & best Field Ambulance we have yet taken over from. Estrées Anchnet, & in all accounts & in good order. JWP	*A.op 36.23 W.2.a.2.8.
"	July 27th		Ordered roll-call for 6-30. Everyone properly issued. Spent whole day cleaning up & replenishing. Started new cook pits, wiring pits etc. JWP	
"	28th		Inspected all Sanitary Controls. 2 1/2 Primary from 1/5 London F.Amb. 3 collected from 37 & 8 in 7 & 49 & Field Ambs at Pies-le-Vrit. O.S.M.S. visited the Ambulance & I emphasize the importance of unit inspection. Visited tent St Etoi in afternoon to inspect advanced dressing station. Paid the Post station a visit in the evening. Lt. Bryan returned from Bus-be-Bripper with his party of 50 Am. JWP	
"	29th		Visited 7 gen Supplement House already at the Advanced Dressing Station	", Divisional Rest Station	from the Station. Road-cutting party.	
"	30th Sun.		Church Parade 9 o am. Conference of O.S.C. Field Ambulance & R.T.n.Si officers occupy the Village. A & S Highlanders & S. African infantry. The Division has now been a complete year in France. JWP	
"	31st Mon.	12-0 noon	Usual work at Advanced Dressing Station. Very few wounded coming in in this sector. Patients showing at H.Q. the Unit = 1/H. Pt:; Child came on strength this Unit vice Lt. O'Donnell attached 103 Bdy/f. JWP	

2353 Wt. W2544/1454. 700,000 5/15 D. D. & L. A.D.S.S./Forms/C. 2118.

Army Form C. 2118.

WAR DIARY
or
INTELLIGENCE SUMMARY.

(Erase heading not required.)

Instructions regarding War Diaries and Intelligence Summaries are contained in F. S. Regs., Part II. and the Staff Manual respectively. Title pages will be prepared in manuscript.

Place	Date	Hour	Summary of Events and Information	Remarks and references to Appendices
Ecoivres-Anzin	July 31st		General Appreciation.	

During the last fortnight the Ambulance has been much on the move. All accessories e.g. Books, Extra equipment collected for the Battle on the original Divisional front, Dressing Ambul. Stats. Red Cross equipment was found valuable to carry 2 Lorry's in stores in a timber wagon. Their transport total equipment was found valuable to carry 2 Lorry's in stores then when moving from Coy to Coy.

invaluable.

The unit seems worked here smoothly than when moving from Coy to Coy.

All officers carried out their duties well, especially was the work of Lt. Q.M. Clahan good.

On the present pattern over from 47th Division.

Evacuation of wounded from the front line of the Advanced Dressing Station during ☆ Augst 51 Q
particular difficulties Supplies & waters are carried on a light railway from Roclincourt Line # 40000 F.8.) 3.5.
by Inf. subs. ⊕ Wounded can be returned on the empty trucks, the distance being about ⊕ " "
2 to 2½ miles. There is most of interest — Sketches for arrival and but protection in F.6.a.4.
case of shell charge appears poor. We can be half of a Top cellar at the afternoon. *F.4.) 8.7.
Dressing station in cd/g of Cpl Chilling other accommodation is roughly for 50 to 60 patients

Excellent. 3 large Dugouts each holding 50 to 10 patients. Besides this there is a good
1 for each - Staff, Equipment stores, & Stewards Store. There is a cool dry room for a stophaven.
I also used as a C of E Canteen. The Soil is Clay upon chalk, drainage of Ecoivres works to
be got good. Transport is Schno & the hospital grounds & to company drinking water had to be obtained
3 miles away in Sanchin - Egal

J W Paters
Capt RAMC
O.C. 50th Fd Ambt

37ᵗʰ Div.

50 Fᵈ Amb / Vol II

Confidential

War Diary

of

O.C 50ᵗʰ Field Ambulance

From 1ˢᵗ August 1916 to 31ˢᵗ August 1916

Volume 13.

Aug 1916

WAR DIARY or INTELLIGENCE SUMMARY

Army Form C. 2118.

by Capt. W. R. Pitcherson
O.C. 50th Field Amb.

Place	Date	Hour	Summary of Events and Information	Remarks and references to Appendices
STREE-CAUCHIE	Aug 1st		Visited A.D.S. at 12-30 where I found 2 R.A.M.C. on the return from visiting "Wormoost Post." Walked along the Advanced Post with Lieut. Forrer. On inspection the Wormoost Dug-out was found to be totally inadequate for the purposes of taking stretcher cases, owing to its steep entry steps, & interior drainage. Also found "relief post" left unprotected from St Eloi & unnecessarily... [illegible] high up by a dangerous shelter. The position of the posts is as follows: Relief Post * magneto exp. point St. Eloi about 1½ miles. Rough road "point C" a crossroad ⊙ could be used by motor ambulances. From here to the Wormoost Post is a "Bad walk" & see it a little need trench Advanced Post † On the Arras – Bethune Rd. Very exposed to direct machine gun fire, & observation from Vimy Ridge. On my return & report of conditions was sent to A.D.M.S. with suggestion that Engineers might supply materials, & lumber, that Infantry fatigue party take large numbers of R.E. field ambulance stretchers on Advanced Dressing Station & Assembly. At front St Eloi Personnel kept there is 2 officers & N.C.Os & 15 R.A.M. (2 Motor Ambs: 3 wheel stretchers) Equipment 1 F.M.B. 1 F.S.P. Dressings. Accommodation 60 lying cases; 40 in a barn on the setting; 10 lying, 10 sitting, in Cellars. At Relief Post – 2 men. At Advanced Post 10 men & 1 N.C.O. Accommodation. 20 – 15 – 5 lying cases in 8 Dug-outs. At Reg't Ad.Post in Zouave Valley. 4 P.M. stretchers for duty at Regimental M.O. Sick Evacuation by push walk on wheel stretchers when no Chillies. Returned by Communication Trench At night by Light Railway to Front St Eloi. It would appear possible to bring Motor Ambulance up to Advanced Post via La Targette Village. but this has not been found necessary yet. S.N.B.W. Nouville – conveyed by Light Line Light Railway from front St Eloi.	* Ref. M/s/51.C. 1,000 F.4.c.6.2. ⊙ F.4.0.2.3 † Aug 36. c. 1,000 S.25.6.9.3

WAR DIARY
INTELLIGENCE SUMMARY

Army Form C. 2118.

Instructions regarding War Diaries and Intelligence Summaries are contained in F.S. Regs., Part II. and the Staff Manual respectively. Title pages will be prepared in manuscript.

(Erase heading not required.)

Place	Date	Hour	Summary of Events and Information	Remarks and references to Appendices
ESTREE-CAUCHIE	Aug 2.		Visits A.D.S. & Divisional Rest Station.	
"	Aug 3rd		Proceeded to Advanced Dressing Station & thence with A.D.M.S. & Capt: Dillon, A.P.M. & Capt Power's "Philosopher" From three parties proceeded via "Orchard Avenue" & "Cromwell Road". These were inspected. Sanitation of units found satisfactory. Cd Cook houses stocked at Gourre Valley. Visits trenches at front line trenches & returned by "Essex" Avenue & "Alarm Bridge" - Indies End. Visits front line French. From Tree 2 "Hospital Corner" & on to which a 91st F.Amb: have an Advanced Post. Red Cross people from D.Sonner delivered stores Corvee Ag: Scotrain; via "Villers-au-bois". Station during afternoon.	
"	Aug 4th		Colo: Pot: & Sa.D.n.g visits the Ambulance & paid visit to Divisional Rest Station. Also O.C. 49th F.Amb:	
"	Aug 5th		Capt: Way, R.O. C.H.O. & Capt: Williams visited Zouave Valley "Troops" Animal Inspections. Pt: Power's detailed to 98th Sick of 182 Tunnelling Coy. during absence (Sick) of R.M.O. to that unit.	
"	Aug 6th Sun:		Lt: MacRae & Lt: Bryson under tour of trenches to learn the inundation. R.A. & Q.M.G. visits Ambulance.	
"	Aug 7th		Capt: Clowes proceeded to Advanced Dressing Station & relieved Capt: Dillon. Lieut: Pierce. Relieved Capt: Clowes at Divisional Rest Station. Can.Court. Lieut: Bryson relieved Lieut: O'Donnell at M.O. 27th Northumberland Fusiliers at Villers au Bois; the latter returning Sick was admitted & 49th F.Amb'. Visit from A.D.M.S. in afternoon. A German Aeroplane flew over the lines at about 7 p.m. dropping [?] & [?] Arouse suspicion of Allies in minds of peasants.	
"	Aug 8th		Col: Watson D.C. 18th (F&I) Fld Amb came to bid 2 N.R. for thankfulness. Why we are given 28 days Field Punishment No. 1. This is the first time in the history of the unit & has been required. Rot: F.Smith A.D.S. visited & approved Saluting [?] with the Ambulance.	

Army Form C. 2118.

WAR DIARY
or
INTELLIGENCE SUMMARY.
(Erase heading not required.)

Place	Date	Hour	Summary of Events and Information	Remarks and references to Appendices
ESTREE-CAUCHIE	Aug 9th		Capt: Dillon left the Field Ambulance for England, having completed 2 years service. His Majesty the King passed through front St-Eloi this afternoon. Lt-Col: Usinar & Major Murray S. African Fd Amb; called to see the Amb: in course of possibly taking over.	
" "	Aug 10th		Lieut: Child relieved Lt: Baker at Advanced Dressing Station. The following officers visited the Ambulance: ADMS 37th Division. ADMS 9th Division. ADVS 3rd Division. O.C. Train 33rd Division. Germans adopt ruse of sending Boys over into Allies lines which return often with bombs & regts: on collars. Lorings reports as having fallen & the Stations.	
" "	Aug 11th		Visited ADMS & Advanced Dressing Station to arrange transfer of probable Drove back to Bruay. Visited Paramount to see S. African Field Ambulance. Capt: F.B. Nicholls (R) arrived during afternoon & later over charge of the Unit, which was and carried out.	

WAR DIARY or INTELLIGENCE SUMMARY

Capt. T. B. NICHOLLS R.A.M.C.
O.C. 50th Field Ambulance
August 1916
Army Form C. 2118.
(4)

Place	Date	Hour	Summary of Events and Information	Remarks and references to Appendices
ESTREE CAUCHIE	11/8/16		Took over command of Unit from Capt. M.W. PATERSON - Newcastle Capt. Rennie (Res.)	JBN
-do-	12/8/16		Inspected A.D.S. at Mt. ST ELOI, the Divisional Rest Station at CAVCOURT. Everything in order. Capt. J.J.H FERGUSON- RAMC (TC) joins for duty from No.1.C.C.S. C.O's parade. Orders received from A.D.M.S. 37th Division for the unit to proceed to BRUAY on 14th. D.R.S evacuates, personnel & patients joining H.Q.	JBN
-do-	13/8/16		A.D.S. handed over to 25th F.A. Personnel reports H.Q. Patients transferred from D.R.S to BRUAY by cars of No 8 M.A.C. under charge of Capt. C.J.B. WAY. Advance party under Lieut. A.W. BAKER left for BRUAY. Patients in Ambulance Main Dressing Station left from BRUAY in cars of the Unit. Lieut F.A O'DONNELL (TC) joines to duty.	JBN
-do-	14/8/16		Unit left for BRUAY at 6 a.m. arrives at 9 a.m. Route ESTREE CAUCHIE, GAUCHIN-LE-GAL, REBRUEVE, HOUDAIN, BRUAY. Thwown discipline was very good.	JBN

Army Form C. 2118.

WAR DIARY
or
INTELLIGENCE SUMMARY. 50th F.A.
(Erase heading not required.) Aug 1916. (5)

Instructions regarding War Diaries and Intelligence Summaries are contained in F. S. Regs., Part II. and the Staff Manual respectively. Title pages will be prepared in manuscript.

Place	Date	Hour	Summary of Events and Information	Remarks and references to Appendices
BRUAY.	14/8/16		Party of 5 N.C.O's men under command of Lieut. R.T. MACLAREN detailed for duty with O/c Forest Control. FOREST of NIEPPE. JBC	
-do-	16/8/16		2 N.CO's, 10 men, two motor Ambulances detailed for duty with IV Corps Scouts at PERNES. JBC	
-do-	19/8/16		Duplicate copies of War Diaries for March — July 1916 sent to O/c Recds for Safe Custody. Two men reinforcements arrived. JBC	
-do-	20/8/16		Inspected detachment in Forest of NIEPPE. Sanitation was not satisfactory. JBC	
-do-	21/8/16		Orders re sanking separticles. No M/097688 Pte DUNCAN G.R. A.S.C. met with an accident when riding a motor cycle — admitted to 1st South African F.A. evacuated to No 6 C.C.S. a couple of training in the ambulance deemed advisable. JBC	
-do-	22/8/16		Capt. E.S. CLOWES of this unit evacuated Sick to No 22 C.C.S. JBC	
-do-	23/8/16		Capt. J.H. FERGUSON attached for temporary duty with 6th Lincoln Regt. V	

WAR DIARY or INTELLIGENCE SUMMARY

50th F.A. 37th Div.
August 1916.
(6)

Army Form C. 2118

Place	Date	Hour	Summary of Events and Information	Remarks and references to Appendices
BRUAY	24/8/16		Capt. A.W. BAKER wants 14 Days Special leave. JBC	
	25/8/16		Officer details to inspect Sanitation of 37th D.S.C. dept. Tramwaiters	
			to A.D.M.S.	
	26/8/16		1 Man evacuated sick. JBC	
	27/8/16		Applies to authority to hand in Bulvessa lanterns of the Equipment as they have been found to be useless. JBC	
	29/8/16		Wrote to A.D.M.S. stating that extra huts are necessary if this site is to be used during the winter. Duties of orderly officer defined. No 38685 Sergt-Major MEDLOCK G.A. reports to duty from 49 F.A. Our Bearer section admitted evacuees to no 22 C.C.S. JBC	
	30/8/16		One N.C.O. evacuated sick. Lieut. S. CHILD details on temporary duty with the IV Corps Schools at PERNES. I inspected the detachment there.	
	31/8/16		Nothing further to report.	

JB Mionolo Major R.A.M.C.
O.C. 50th F.A.

WAR DIARY

of

Major T. B. Nicholls R. A. M. C.

Commanding 50th Field Ambulance.

From 1st September 1916 to 30th September 1916.

Vol: XIV

Army Form C. 2118

WAR DIARY
or
INTELLIGENCE SUMMARY

September 1916 (1)

(Erase heading not required.)

Instructions regarding War Diaries and Intelligence Summaries are contained in F.S. Regs., Part II. and the Staff Manual respectively. Title Pages will be prepared in manuscript.

Place	Date	Hour	Summary of Events and Information	Remarks and references to Appendices
BRUAY			War Diary of O.C. 50th Field Ambulance, 37th Division. September 1916.	
	1/9/16		Court of Enquiry as to how No.M/097688 Pte Duncan D. came to damage Motor Bicycle. The man was found to have damaged the bicycle by negligence and was awarded 14 days F.P. No.1 and ordered to pay £1. towards the cost of repairing the bicycle. Major R.A.M.C. Commanding 50th Field Ambulance.	
"	3/9/16		One man evacuated sick. One man joined.	
"	7/9/16		Army Form M.T./393 for Sergeant Walker H.W. submitted, as this N.C.O. is desirous of joining the Royal Flying Corps.	
"	8/9/16		Inspection by G.O.C. 37th Division. Captain A.W. Baker returned from leave. Captain J.J.H. Ferguson returned from temporary duty with the 8th Lincoln Regiment.	
"	10/9/16		Captain J.J.H. Ferguson proceeded on 14 days leave on completion of his one year's contract.	
"	11/9/16		One man evacuated sick. The following promotions were made on the authority of D.D.M.S. IV Corps. No.36825 Lance Corpl Townsley H.A. to be Corporal. No.38144 Lance Corpl Gallery D.B. to be Corporal. The following appointments were made. No. 39149 Private Weston T. to Lance Corporal. No. 37008 Private Blight F. to Lance Corporal.	
"	12/9/16		Inspection by A.D.M.S. 37th Division.	
"	16/9/16		One man rejoined from No. 6 C.C.S.	
"	17/9/16		Lieut R.T. MacLaren proceeded to 37th Divisional Train for duty. Advance party under Lieut Mercer proceeded to BARLIN.	

Army Form C. 2118

WAR DIARY
or
INTELLIGENCE SUMMARY

50th Field Ambulance,

September 1916 (2)

(Erase heading not required.)

Instructions regarding War Diaries and Intelligence Summaries are contained in F.S. Regs., Part II. and the Staff Manual respectively. Title Pages will be prepared in manuscript.

Place	Date	Hour	Summary of Events and Information	Remarks and references to Appendices
Bruay	18/9/16.		Unit moved to BARLIN. Left BRUAY 10.15.a.m. arrived BARLIN 12. noon. Took over from 3rd Naval Field Ambulance, who relieved this Unit at Bruay.	
BARLIN	19/9/16		Inspection by A.A.Q.M.G. and A.D.M.S. 37th Division. A.S.C. C3¹⁰(R.M.)D.S.C.	
BARLIN	20/9/16		No. 032830 Private HOULDIN G. brought in dead. Post Mortem performed by order of the A.D.M.S. Cause of death found to be "acute alcoholic poisoning", by rum. Three men proceeded on leave.	
"	21/9/16		Captain C.J.B. Way proceeded to 48th Field Ambulance for temporary duty.	
"	23/9/16		Inspection by A.D.M.S. 37th Division. Lieut S. Child proceeded to 10th Battalion Yorks & Lancs Regiment for temporary duty.	
"	24/9/16		Commanding Officer's Inspection Parade. Conference of O's C. Field Ambulances at A.D.M.S's Office. Captain J.J.H. Ferguson returned from leave	
"	25/9/16		Gas Alarm at 10.40.p.m. The standing orders for Gas Alarm were carried out without a hitch.	
"	26/9/16		Inspection by A.D.M.S.	
"	27/9/16		Commanding Officer and Captain Paterson visited the A.D.S. of 49th Field Ambulance and made a tour of the trenchs and the area cleared by this A.D.S.	
"	28/9/16		"Turn-out" Competition for the Horse Transport of this Unit. Prizes were given by the Officers for the best in each class.	
"	29/9/16		Inspection by A.A.Q.M.G. and G.S.O. (1) 37th Division. Intimation received from A.D.M.S. 37th Division that Medical Officers of Field Ambulances are to be reduced to seven in number. Captain A.W. Baker was chosen to be sent away when the reduction comes into force.	
"	30/9/16		Nothing to report.	

Major R.A.M.C.
Commanding 50th Field Ambulance.

Army Form C. 2118

WAR DIARY
or
INTELLIGENCE SUMMARY
(Erase heading not required.)

50th Field Ambulance,
September 1916.   (3)

Instructions regarding War Diaries and Intelligence Summaries are contained in F. S. Regs., Part II. and the Staff Manual respectively. Title Pages will be prepared in manuscript.

Place	Date	Hour	Summary of Events and Information	Remarks and references to Appendices
BRUAY			Summary of work done during the month.	
			New horse standings erected. New incinerator built to dispose of faeces and a system of latrines installed to work with it.	
			Huts covered with tarred felting and ramp kettle stand built in cookhouse.	
BARLIN			Entire surface of camp metalled with slag, about 200 hundred yeards of road also metalled. Cookhouse built, soak-pits dug, new system of latrines with incinerator to burn faeces erected. Ablution room built.	
			The Unit has worked under considerable difficulties during the month. One Officer and fifty other ranks were detached to work in the Forest of Nieppe. A further detachment of twelve N.C.O.'s and men were sent to the IV Corps Schools at PERNES. Thus a third of the personnel were away from the Unit during the entire month.	
			The G.S. Wagons were detached to work under the R.E. for a fortnight when at B R U A Y.	
			The Unit has been acting as a Divisional Rest Station during the period.	

J B Newalle

Major R.A.M.C.

Commanding 50th Field Ambulance.

140/1815

87th Division

War Diary

of

Major T. B. NICHOLLS. R.A.M.C
Commanding 50th Field Ambulance

From 1st October 1916 To 31st October 1916

VOL. 15

Confidential
Oct. 1916

COMMITTEE FOR THE
MEDICAL HISTORY OF THE WAR
Date -9 DEC. 1916

WAR DIARY or INTELLIGENCE SUMMARY

Army Form C. 2118

50th F.A.

OCT 1916 — ①

Place	Date	Hour	Summary of Events and Information	Remarks and references to Appendices
BARLIN	1/10/16		50th Field Ambulance, 37th Division - October 1916. 3 O.R. Proceeded on leave. Lieut. J.D. MERCER proceeds on leave. O.B. Newcastle. Info. Re:inf. Command 50 F.A.M.	
Do	2/10/16		Capt. C.J.B. WAY returned from 48 F.A. & proceeds to Meer de Nieppe in place of Capt. A.E. BAKER who proceeds to 63" (RN) Div. for duty.	
Do	3/10/16		Capt. J.J.H. FERGUSON proceeded to 9th Dist. for duty. 1 N.C.O. returns from No. 22 COS. 1 man evacuated sick.	
Do	6/10/16		Inspection by A.D.M.S. 37th Div. Return sent to "Q" HQ 37th Div. of Ordnance Stores down during month to 30th September - total value £475 - including water cart £75 - Hutts blanket (personnel & 60 about) Stretchers £31 & Boots £30. The Balance £129 was for expendable stores - a large proportion of which were issued to patients on discharge from Divisional Rest Station.	
Do	7/10/16		Detachment on fatigue at FORET de NIEPPE returned (50 men) & 2 C. been sent in relief. This party had been away from the unit since Aug 15/16.	
Do	8/10/16		4 O.R. proceeds on leave. Capt M.W. PATERSON awarded 7 days sick leave.	

WAR DIARY or INTELLIGENCE SUMMARY

Army Form C. 2118

503 A. Oct 1916

Place	Date	Hour	Summary of Events and Information	Remarks and references to Appendices
BERTIN	8/10/16	Cont'd	Capt J.V.O. ANDREW joined for duty 8th Division on completion of the test from out left. A.S.C. (H.T.) of the unit. All medical completion to the brigade were different. Ballot a very good class. No 40250 Sergt WALKER. R.H.W. was interviewed by G.O.C. 63" July Bde and his suitability for a commission in R.F.C. a was passed as suitable.	
Do.	9/10/16		Capt. C.J.B. WBY returns from Inér du Notpe having handed over command at Arlequeve in Itargue tree to an officer of 4th Middlesex Regt.	
Do.	10/10/16		(Capt. H.N. STAFFORD (SR) reports for duty from No 6 C.C.S. She was discharged reports from 73rd Field Ambulance. Capt. J.V.O. ANDREW - proceeds to temporary duty 4th D.M. Capt. H.D. GOUGH admits to duty from 73rd Field Ambulance Sergt. S. CHILD returns from Leave. Lieut J.D. MERCER returns from Leave + proceeds to 94 g A. to Temporary duty	
Do	11/10/16		Lieut J.A. O'DONNEL proceeds to 2nd E.D.S.A. for duty.	
Do	12/10/16		Capt. H.N. STAFFORD attended demonstration at Army Gas School. Inspection by G.O.C. 37th Bdr. + A.D.M.S. Issues 200 sand bags unit to be Kitchener Memorial stores	
Do	13/10/16		Inspection latrines, Kit inspection of all ranks	
Do	14/10/16		Inspection latrines - Capt J.D. MERCER returns from 4g AmB - Capt J.V.O. ANDREW returns from 2gts in Sept. All patients evacuated, none received.	

WAR DIARY or INTELLIGENCE SUMMARY

Army Form C. 2118

No. 50694. Oct 16 (3)

Place	Date	Hour	Summary of Events and Information	Remarks and references to Appendices
BARLIN	15/10/16		Orders received to proceed to FRESNICOURT. Left BARLIN 2 p.m. arrived 3.45 p.m. Q.O.R. proceeded on leave	
FRESNICOURT	16/10/16		Detachment from Corps Schools at PERNES rejoined. Left for DIÉVAL at 11 a.m. arrived 4 p.m.	
DIÉVAL	17/10/16		Capt M.W. PATERSON returned from leave	
DIÉVAL	18/10/16		Left for ST. MICHEL en TERNOISE 10 a.m. arrived 1 p.m. A Draws Inspected. Fatigue party from forest de Nièppe rejoined. All the unit uses the Baths at Rod Napta Camp ST POL.	
ST MICHEL	19/10/16		Rearranged waggon loads - revised list of sections a holding of officers & sections as under. A Section - Major J.B. NICHOLLS. B Section - Capt. M.W. PATERSON. C Sect. Capt. C.B. WAY. Capt. H.N. STAFFORD. Capt. J.V.O. ANDREW. Lieut. J.D. MERCER. Lieut. S. CHILD. Lieut. r.Qm. M.W. COLOHAN.	

Army Form C. 2118

WAR DIARY
or
INTELLIGENCE SUMMARY

(Erase heading not required.)

50th 3 A Oct /16

Instructions regarding War Diaries and Intelligence Summaries are contained in F. S. Regs., Part II. and the Staff Manual respectively. Title Pages will be prepared in manuscript.

Place	Date	Hour	Summary of Events and Information	Remarks and references to Appendices
ST MICHEL	20/10/16		Left ST MICHEL 9 a.m. arrives MONCHEAUX 11.30 a.m. Passes G.O.C. 35th Bde. in line of route & pays usual compliments.	
MONCHEAUX	21/10/16		Left MONCHEAUX 7 a.m. arrives BRETEL 2 p.m. Staff Sgt S/ SMITH to be P.M.S. Cap. order 35 dt 7/10/16. Left BRETEL at 8 a.m. arrives SARTON 10.30 a.m.	
BRETEL	22/10/16			
SARTON	23/10/16		Left at 11.45 p.m. for BERTRANCOURT – orders received in line of march to go to ACHEUX in lieu – arrives 4 p.m. 10 OR details for duty at No 3 CCS. Lieut B. O'NEILL detailed for duty at 27 CCS. Capt. J v O ANDREW, Tent Subdivision of B Sect. Detailed for duty at V Corps Collecting Station. ACHEUX.	views of Hastings 37 62 Div
ACHEUX	24/10/16		Capt. H.M STAFFORD detailed for duty at Combined Main Dressing Station at VARENNES. Inspection by A.D.M.S. Bearer Subdivision of A/B Sect. under Lieut J.D MERCER & Capt M.W PATERSON detailed (the rest) in reserve to detail A.D.M.S 2 W Div at BERTRANCOURT.	

Army Form C. 2118.

WAR DIARY
or
INTELLIGENCE SUMMARY.   50k J.A.   Oct '16 (5)

(Erase heading not required.)

Instructions regarding War Diaries and Intelligence Summaries are contained in F.S. Regs., Part II. and the Staff Manual respectively. Title pages will be prepared in manuscript.

Place	Date	Hour	Summary of Events and Information	Remarks and references to Appendices
ACHEUX	27/10/16	Cont.	When required. Bearer subdivision t/O section leader Capt. C.J.B. WAY Remained billeted & report to Lieut. Col. D.P. WATSON to hand up Divisional Bearer Company when required. A.D.M.S. two D.D.R. called to arrange about transport.	
ACHEUX	28/10/16		Lieut E.F.R. ALFORD (T.C.) reported for duty. Received orders to proceed to ARQUÈVES at 4.30 pm. Packed up – marched off at 5 pm arrived 6 pm.	✓✓
ARQUÈVES	29/10/16		One man transferred to No 2. Walking Column to duty.	
	29/10/16		Equipment overhauls & repaired. Left ARQUÈVES 2 P.M. Arrive SARTON 4 pm.	
SARTON	30/10/16		Left SARTON. 1.30 – arrive BRETEL SUR-SOMME. CAPTAIN. STAFFORDS detached from Bearer Station. Capt. J.V.O HOMAN & Tent Subdivision of B sect. reported from Corps Collecting Station.	✓✓
SARTON	31/10/16		Lt. R.D. M. M. W. COLDHAM proceeded to 10 days special leave. Precolls. Walsrane. Commanding 50th Field Ambulance.	

2353 Wt. W2514/1454 700,000 5/15 D. D. & L.   A.D.S.S./Forms/C. 2118.

31st North Midland Div.
Vol 14

Confidential

War Diary

— of —

Major T. B. NICHOLLS R.A.M.C.

Commanding No. 50 Field Ambulance

COMMITTEE FOR THE
MEDICAL HISTORY OF THE WAR
Date −3 JAN. 1917

To 30 NOV 1916.

M

VOL. XVI

From 1 NOV 1916

Army Form C. 2118.

WAR DIARY
or
INTELLIGENCE SUMMARY.
(Erase heading not required.)

Instructions regarding War Diaries and Intelligence Summaries are contained in F. S. Regs., Part II. and the Staff Manual respectively. Title pages will be prepared in manuscript.

Place	Date	Hour	Summary of Events and Information	Remarks and references to Appendices
BRETEL 1/11/16			50th Field Ambulance, 37th Division, November 1916.	
			One Motor cycle (broken front forks) exchanged – O/B Melville. Major Rennie Commanding 50/15 Field Ambulance	
BRETEL	3/11/16		Colonel A. TOWNSLEY to interview A.D.M.S. as to his suitability for a commission. Return of Mules called for by 'Q'. It is proposed to utilise some of them to augment Pack transport of Infantry. Should this be done it will unnecessitate the Ambulance 2BR	
– Do –	4/11/16		Visits the A.D.M.S. 1/1	
– Do –	7/11/16		Col. H.A. TOWNSLEY interviewed by G.O.C. 112th Infy. Bde. & handed an outline to a Commission. Large amount of abandoned stores found in BRETEL. Salvage Officer, 37th Divn. notified. 1/1	
– Do –	8/11/16		Field day. Bearer subdivisions exercises in a scheme in an advance 1/1	
	9/11/16		Night operations. The same scheme in evolution carried out. Commencing at 8 p.m.	
– Do –	10/11/16		W. Day – Field day – none of his we scheme back from 11 am to 3.0 pm Lt. Qr. Mr. M.W. COLCHAM Returns from leave. One man rejoins from C.C.S. 1/1	

Army Form C. 2118.

WAR DIARY
or
INTELLIGENCE SUMMARY.   50th F.A. Nov '16   (2)
(Erase heading not required.)

Place	Date	Hour	Summary of Events and Information	Remarks and references to Appendices
BRETEL	11/11/16		X Bay. Walores representatives at 112th F.A. H.Q. Conference at office of A.D.M.S. R.A.M.C operation order No 19 received.	
BRETEL	12/11/16		Y day. Unit left at 1.30 pm arrived LOUVENCOURT 5.45 pm. Tent Subdivision of B Section proceeded to Corps Collecting Station under Capt. J.V.O ANDREW. Ambulance cars sent to follow 112th Inf. Bde as large numbers of men were reported to be falling out. Only four however could be found. A.D.M.S orders us to have 2 Bearer Subdivisions in readiness.	
LOUVENCOURT			Bearer Subdivisions of B Section under Capt. O.J.B. WAY & Capt. M.W. PATERSON respectively detached to the 112 Inf. Bde who are going into action. Marches off between 10th L.N. Lancs Regt at 5.30 pm. Orders to detail 4 Amb. Cars to relieve congestion at Colin CAMPS. A.D.Q.M.G called. Capt. M.W. PATERSON depart. He was with 2nd Division.	
- do -	14/11/16		Two Horsed Ambulances & 4 G.S. Waggons started to Bely with 83rd Division Collecting Station	

Army Form C. 2118.

WAR DIARY
or
INTELLIGENCE SUMMARY.

50 T F.A. Nov' 16   (3)

(Erase heading not required.)

Instructions regarding War Diaries and Intelligence Summaries are contained in F. S. Regs., Part II. and the Staff Manual respectively. Title pages will be prepared in manuscript.

Place	Date	Hour	Summary of Events and Information	Remarks and references to Appendices
LOUVENCOURT	15/11/16		No. M/2/055079 Pte WELLMAN, A.S.C. to assumed the motor cycle orderly duties. Left leave for OLARTAYE 1.30 pm - arrived 2.45 pm to take over VI Corps Post Station from 2nd Field Ambulance 63rd (Royal Naval) Division	
CLAIRFAYE	16/11/16		C.R.S. taking over complete. Capt. H.N. STAFFORD Unaries for duty with 2nd/1 mres Bearing Station at THE COOKERS (map 57B Q 29.a.4.5) Six Motor Ambulances sent to 48th F.A. for duty at Main Dressing Station.	Appendix I
do	17/11/16		Capt M.W. PATTERSON I bearers of B Section returned to H.Q. his hat attached one Casualty No. 28112 Pte O.A.D.M. slightly wounded (shell in head - remained at duty Capt C I B. WAY I Bearers of C sect un returned. His report attached. The Casualties No. 39789 Pte JERMYN. J. No. 40592 Pte HAYES T. (wounded) evacuated. Capt J.V.O ANDREW & Tent Subdivision of B section returned from Corps Collecting Station. Six Reinforcements arrived.	Appendix II
do	18/11/16	2am	Lieut J.D MERCER & Bearers of A section Joined 112th Bde at HAMEL. Horses sent up in Sup. to Motor Ambulances returning to A.D.S. on foot. Nothing should be hear. A This B.k Sta work covering the evacuation of 90th W=8th Bde for the work done by the Bearers.	
do	19/11/16	2pm	Capt M.W. PATTERSON & Bearers of B sect left to clear 116 Bde. 1 N.C.O regimentals from 1 MT A.S.A warrant - disc. Inspection by A.D.M.S V Corps. A.D.M.S B.D.K. Bath.	

WAR DIARY or INTELLIGENCE SUMMARY.

Army Form C. 2118.

50th F.A. Nov/16 (4)

Place	Date	Hour	Summary of Events and Information	Remarks and references to Appendices
LHIRFAYE	20/11/16		Notified that Lieut. J.D. MERCER was sent to 10th N Lancs Regt to replace their M.O. – acknowledgements	
–Do–	21/11/16		Lieut. J.D. Mercer evacuated sick (? Paratyphoid) Capt. H.N. STAFFORD sent to replace him.	
–Do–	22/11/16		70 sick Pony with Thrush Biontrata admitted to polyf. All Carriers obstinut. Inspection by D.D.U.S. & Capt. Two Mules Influenza. Injuries. Joined 4 & 8th F.A. No 2220B 1st A.M. N.H.S.H. – 32d Squad. R.F.C. brought in dead Postman in performed by Capt. N.v. O ANDREW. Cause of death. Alcoholic Poisoning. Dictated Room. Baths completed for Corps Restations – capacity 150 men per view. Due to no laundry available to obtaining clean underclothes.	
–Do–	24/11/16		Lieut. H.R. GRELLET joined for duty from No 2 General Hospital. Three WOLSELEY Cars sent to Supply Column to be exchanged for SIDDELEY-DEASY type. A/Cpno. 35th D.S.C. Collect.	
–Do–	25/11/16		Refenenies – Two officers & 2 Tent-subdivisions of 21st F.A. arrived to commence testing over.	

Army Form C. 2118.

WAR DIARY
or
INTELLIGENCE SUMMARY. 50th F.A. Nov '16

(5)

(Erase heading not required.)

Place	Date	Hour	Summary of Events and Information	Remarks and references to Appendices
CLAIRFAYE	26/11/16		Capt M.W. PATERSON & B Sect Bearers returned this report is attached. No casualties.	Appendix III
	27/4/16		Capt J.V.O. ANDREW left for V Corps Trench Mortar School at VAL HEREUX in chief if absent J.P. DOUGLAS who joined this unit in his place. Remainder of 21st F.A arrives - V.C.R. Stn handed over 569 Patients	2L
-Do-			Left CLAIRFAYE 8 am. arrived LOUVENCOURT at 5pm. 112 Fd Hy RDC orders in which we were ordered to leave at 10.30 am did not reach me till 12.45 pm owing to delay in D.R.L.S. which has been very interesting lately - probably owing to bad roads. No 37749 Cpl GORDON to warded sergeant - auth DD MS V Corps 406/1629/16 Dates 25/11/16. 3 O.R. proceeded on leave.	JB [signature]
LOUVENCOURT	28/11/16			
-Do-	30/11/16		Left LOUVENCOURT at 9.30 am arrived at VAL DE MAISON 2.30pm. I was sent by D Brms V th Corps. Do unit marched under command of Capt M W PATERSON. At 11.15 July B Ds was marching in two groups. 3 horse Ambulances in charge of Lt GRELLET followed one half 6 fr. Motor Ambulances indident DOUGLAS followed the other. About 100 men were carried in all.	JB [signature]

WAR DIARY
or
INTELLIGENCE SUMMARY. 50th D.A. Nov 16

Army Form C. 2118.

(Erase heading not required.)

Place	Date	Hour	Summary of Events and Information	Remarks and references to Appendices

Supplementary Notes

1/ The officers [to the] observers beorins report, that owing to no French maps were issued, they had the greatest of difficulty in finding their way about especially in the dark.

2/ The DODGE & M.S. Motor Cycles proved unsuitable for the purpose of intercommunication between Batteries for following reasons.

 1/ Front fork springs are not strong enough — Both bicycles had their front forks broken during the month.

 2/ Motor cycle tyres. Every time a stop has to be made the rider has to start by running. One man was exhausted, the others returned from a short run exhausted.

 3/ Great trouble was caused by short-circuits owing to the least mud & insufficient protection of the plugs.

 4/ The mud guards had to be removed as there was not sufficient clearance between them & the wheels. When the mud was sticky the wheels became bogged up.

O.S.Grenville Malahan
Commanding 50th Field Ambulance

Appendix ~~VIII~~ I

Report of operations carried out by
B. Section (Bearer Subdivision) 50th Field Amb.
Nov 13th to 17th
1916.

To
O.C.
50th Field Ambulance.

Sir,
 I have the honour to report the following operations carried out by B. Section 50th F. Amb. from Nov 13th to 17th. At 5 p.m. on 13th inst. B & C Sections with Capt. Bray, under my command, left Louvencourt following the 112th Brigade to Bertrancourt via Bus. From Bertrancourt the Sections returned to Bus finding billets at 10.30 p.m. At 9.30 a.m. 14th inst. on receipt of a wire from Bde. Headquarters I proceeded with B Section to the RED HOUSE Mailly, leaving Capt. Bray at Bus in charge of C Section. I reported, as instructed, to Lieut. Col. ROBINSON, O.C. 40th Field Amb. and 7.30 a.m. I proceeded from this place (Red House) to point K.33.c (Ref. Map 57 D 40,000) known as the SUCRERIE & came under the command of Capt. BOURNE-PRICE who was in charge of bearers. With CAPT. MARRACK as guide the Section proceeded to the "WHITE CITY" where I gained touch with the 6th Bedford Regt. & found the Regimental Medical Officer. The Section proceeded to collect wounded from the trenches on the old front line, returning with them to WHITE CITY. Patients belonged to the ESSEX Regt. & trenches used were "MOUNTJOY," "CHATHAM," "TOURNAI." At about 4 p.m. when in "CHATHAM" trench the enemy put up a heavy barrage & CAPT. MARRACK leading into 4th AVENUE further progress was deemed inadvisable, & shelter was found in an old dugout. Acting on a report that wounded lay out in the German first & second lines, after about 45 mins. Capt. Marrack advised to push on

in spite of the barrage, as darkness was rapidly approaching, & following his example the whole party proceeded over the top of the trenches towards the German lines taken the day previous. Although quite in the open, & experiencing the nauseous fumes of Cordite, as well as the frequent explosions, the behaviour of the men was splendid, & the German lines were entered after much difficulty, with barbed wire, mud & shell-holes. During all this time the barrage of the enemy was intense, added to which a German machine gun swept the crest of the hill from time to time. Regimental Aid Posts of the 7th K.R.R. & of the H.L.I. were found in the deep enemy dug-outs, some of which were were 40ft: deep & over 100 yds: in length. Wounded men, many of whom had been lying out 24 hours, were taken back from this region, & the party once again came under machine-gun fire. It was now approx 6.30 p.m. & Enemy barrage was dying down, but some difficulty was found bringing the cases back in the dark. From White City, Sergt. Jones was sent back with the 3rd Division, while I returned to the "Sucrerie" to report to CAPT. BOURNE-PRICE that many wounded still lay unattended in the German lines & in shell-holes, & to ask for more bearers. Two Sub-divisions of a South Midland F. Amb: in Corps: Reserve, were brought up with 2 officers from Bertrancourt. These I led by "Tournai" over to the German 2nd line trenches, returning with 1st parties overland to the Sucrerie. Meanwhile urgent messages for volunteer bearers had been sent out by the Brigadier occupying a dug-out in "WHITE CITY", & between 10 & 11 p.m. these arrived. I conducted this party with tinker & stretchers, over the same ground to the German lines & cleared all dug-outs as far as possible. Over 120 were evacuated in this way these bearers doing one complete journey to the Sucrerie, a few parties did two. During all this time the

Section under my command and was working between German lines & White City under the direction of Sergt: Jones H.J. & L/Cpl HOLLINGSWORTH. E. They made 4 journeys & carried on through the morning of the 15th inst: under heavy enemy barrage fire.

I desire Sir, to bring to your notice certain N.C.Os and men whose devotion to duty under the most trying conditions deserve recognition. (This list is given in an addendum herewith.) Having shown the volunteer bearers the way of evacuation I picked up the B Section Squads at the White City about dawn. The E. LANCS: Regt: 112th Bde: were proceeding at this moment past "White City" & I was able to gain touch with C Section Bearers, under Capt: Way. After consultation with Capt: BOURNE-PRICE, & after a further carry of 2 Squads to the "Sucrerie" I established an Advanced Post in "CHATHAM" trench, in a dug-out in our old front line, & collected water provisions & dressings here. Utterly fatigued the men now had 3 hours rest & then proceeded to assist wounded walking back from the morning attack, 15th. At 4-30 p.m. I received an order from Capt: BOURNE-PRICE to return with my party to the SUCRERIE, in order to be relieved. I handed over the post in "CHATHAM" trench to CAPT: WAY on leaving. During the operations one Squad was blown over by bursting shell, one man being wounded in the head. At 7-30 p.m. the party returned to "RED-HOUSE" At 9 a.m. 16th inst: party returned to Bertrancourt returning to Head Quarters the Field Ambulance on 17th inst:

I have the honour to be Sir,

Your obedient Servant

J. W. Paterson, Capt: R.A.M.C.
O.C. Bearers Bearers

17/11/16

Appendix II

To O.C. 50th Field Ambulance

Sir

I have the honour to report the following movements of C Section Bearer Sub-division under my command from Nov 13th–17th.

Nov 13th 4 p.m. Marched to BERTRAMCOURT from thence to BUS. We were billeted in huts occupied by No 142 Field Ambulance.

Nov 14th 9 a.m. I Reported to ADMS 3rd Div. who attached me to O.C. 142 Fd Amb for duty temporarily.

3.15 p.m. Proceeded to MAILLY-MAILLET behind 8th East Lancs & 10th Loyal North Lancs. Arrived at 6 p.m. proceeding to billets allotted.

8 p.m. I attempted to obtain information of the medical arrangements from the RED HOUSE & SUCRERIE

Nov 15th 2 a.m. Moved off to trenches. Under orders from Bdg. Gen. Robinson, 112 Bgd, I detailed 4 squads under Staff Sergt. Gillespie to attach themselves to M.O. of the 8th East Lancs. Myself and the remaining 4 squads I placed at the disposal of M.O. of 18 Loyal N. Lancs. We proceeded up 6th Avenue to White City from thence up 4th Avenue to Green Line from which the two Battalions attacked. A Combined Regimental Aid Post was made in Green Line. I assisted the Regimental M.O.'s to dress cases coming in and also detailed some of my bearers to fetch cases who had fallen near Green Line.

About Midday As there were eight stretcher cases, I proceeded with them and about 12 walking wounded back to the Sucrerie a carry of nearly 4 hours. Returning I found Capt. Paterson's dug out in Chatham Trench. As his party was being relieved I made this my head quarters. At dusk we attempted to return to the R.A.P. but were unable to find the way. While waiting for the moon to rise we took 8 cases from the English Line to White City

Nov 16th At 1 a.m. I again attempted to reach the R.A.P. with my squads. Some of the rear squads were taken by an officer of the H.L.I. and divided up Oh little men to 5 of his. There made three carries from German 1st & 2nd line to White City. My men rejoined at 8.30 I reached Green Line but not the R.A.P, having found 5,8th East Lancs stretcher cases. These I [took] to White City.

At 7 a.m. I allowed the men 2 hours rest.

At 9 a.m I attempted to get thro again to the R.A.P. with my bearers but was prevented getting beyond the German 1st line owing to a severe barrage. There were many cases lying in deep dugouts and in shell-holes who had not been attended for 2 or 3 days. The whole of the morning was spent in clearing as many of these as possible to White City.

At 2 p.m. a wire from M.O. i/c 11th Warwicks arrived asking for bearers. I detailed 2 squads under Staff Sergeant Gillespie to proceed. These were not able to reach the Warwicks Aid Post being caught in a barrage - being unable to leave the 1st German line. They returned later with two cases to my Hd. Qrs.

In the afternoon with Pte Hatton I proceeded to the R.A.P. to find out the number of stretcher cases left as help had been promised me. At nightfall as the barrage had lessened I proceeded with my bearers to the R.A.P. taking six of the worst cases back.

Nov. 17th At 2 a.m. I met the Officer in charge of the reserve Bearers and directed him to the R.A.P. The Brigade track having been marked during the evening with tape.

I received orders to proceed to MAILLY-MAILLET when convenient. I made another journey to the R.A.P. but the Reserve bearers had evacuated it. We carried back four cases we found in the open to White City.

At 7 a.m. I proceeded to MAILLY-MAILLET where we rested.

At 12 midday was ordered to rejoin the 50th Field Ambulance at CLAIRFAYE leaving MAILLY at 2 p.m.

4:30 I Arrived at CLAIRFAYE and reported to you.

Sir

I have the honour to be
Your obedient servant

November 18th 1916

[signature]
Captain R.A.M.C.
O i/c Section Bearer Subdivision (S.R.)
50th Field Ambulance

Appendix III

Report of Operations carried out by B Section & later, A Section, 50th Field Ambulance Nov 19th to 26th

1916.

To. O.C.

50th Field Ambulance.

Sir,

Under instructions from you I proceeded with B Section bearers to Varennes, & thence by cars to "THE COOKERS", marching the Section through HAMEL to the "RELIEF POST" Bearer Headquarters [map ref: Q.18.c.5.6. map 57 D 1/40,000] I reported to Capt. EVANS who was in charge of bearers. He directed me to ADVANCED POST. STATION ROAD [Q.12.d.7.3. map 57 D 1/40,000] Here I joined CAPT. BROUGH 49th F. Amb: in charge of bearers. LIEUT: MERCER in charge of A Section bearers 50th Field Amb & LIEUT: RENWICK in charge of 48th Field Amb: bearers. Regimental Medical Officers, of 10th R. Fusiliers & 13th R. Fusiliers. In conjunction with these officers each Brigade of the 37th Division was cleared of wounded by the different Sections of the Ambulances concerned. On the afternoon of my arrival Nov 19th Capt: Donovan. Regt: Medical Officer 10th Royal North Lancs: was wounded, & I replaced him by Lieut Mercer taking over A Section from him. LIEUT: MERCER having been unwell for some days & having a high temperature was evacuated on Nov 21st, his place being taken by Capt STAFFORD, 50th Field Amb: The 111th Brigade being withdrawn on Nov 23rd & 24th 48th Field Amb: bearers withdrawn, & under directions from A.D.M.S. 37th Division I took over command of bearers. On the morning of 25th inst: at dawn 49th Field Amb: Bearers were withdrawn, followed by 50th Field Amb bearers, who returned by was to Varennes, marching back to Headquarters the Ambulance at Clairfaye.

Capt: Austin R.A.M.C. 11th Division arrived at Station Rd with bearers on the evening of Nov 22nd. The 7th Division, 21st Manchester Regt: relieved the Loyal North Lancs: Regt: in the line, on the evening of the 25th inst:

I have the honour to be Sir,
Your obedient Servant,

J.W. Paterson
Capt: R.A.M.C.
O.C. Bearer Sub-division
B Section 50th Field Amb:

26.11.16.

CONFIDENTIAL. Vol 15

War Diary

of

Lieut-Col. J. B. Nicholls - R.A.M.C.
Commanding 50th Field Ambulance.

from December 1st 1916. to December 31st 1916.

(Volume 17.)

COMMITTEE FOR THE
MEDICAL HISTORY OF THE WAR
Date 31 JAN. 1917

Army Form C. 2118.

50th F.A. Dec '16 (1)

WAR DIARY
or
INTELLIGENCE SUMMARY.
(Erase heading not required.)

Place	Date	Hour	Summary of Events and Information	Remarks and references to Appendices
VAL DE MAISON	1/12/16		War diary of Lieut. Col. V.B. NICHOLLS, R.A.M.C. Commanding 50th Field Ambulance 37th Division.	
do	2/12/16		Captain D.H. HADDEN R.A.M.C. (T.O.) joins from No 8 Stationary Hospital. 28 Other Ranks to Divn Inspection by A.D.M.S. 37th Divn & Q.R.E. Lt. S. CHILD left 47 C.C.S; took over temporary charge of 37th Divn. Sanitary Section. Capt. H.N. STAFFORD & 3 Other Ranks proceeded on leave. Capt. D.H. HADDEN detailed for Medical Charge of 10th Bn Royal North Lancs Regt.	
do	3/12/16		C.O's parade - Kit inspection. One man evacuated sick to CCS (No 3)	
do	4/12/16		Training programme commenced consisting of lectures, drill, practical instruction in Nursing Duties and first aid.	
do	6/12/16		A.Duns called. 3 O.R. proceed on leave	
do	7/12/16		No 32268 Q.M. Sergt. ALLCARD T.W. transferred to 74 & 5th Field Ambulance for duty & struck of the strength accordingly. Lieut. H.R. GRELLET detailed for temporary duty with 37th Divisional Train. Vice Capt. R.G. POYSER sick.	
do	8/12/16		Medical Board held to ascertain of A.A.M.S. to occasify P.B. men -	
do	9/12/16		C.R.E. called to inspect a hut being erected	
do	10/12/16		3 O.R. proceed on leave	

Army Form C. 2118.

WAR DIARY
or
INTELLIGENCE SUMMARY. 50th J.A. Decr '16 (2)

(Erase heading not required.)

Place	Date	Hour	Summary of Events and Information	Remarks and references to Appendices
VAL de MAISON	11/12/16		Inspection by G.O.C. 37th Div in rain. Lectures by C.O. to medical officers of 1/12th Inf Bde in water sterilisation. O.B.S.	
Do.	13/12/16	4 O.R. proceed on leave. Unit leaves VAL de MAISON 9 am. arriving BRETEL 12.45 p.m. 9 to now attached to 111 Inf. Bde while on the march. Called on Bde Major to arrange the collection of stragglers. 9 men unfit to march. One Motor Omnibus attached to Unit. One 3 Ton Lorry 75 Blankets, Stretchers &c. Lieut E.F.R. ALFORD details temporary medical charge of the E Lancs Reft.	
BRETEL	14/12/16		Unit marches to NOEUX leaving 9.30 am arriving 3 pm. Inspected on line of march by G.O.C. 37th Div. All men unable to march, the sick were collected before units left. Most of the sick were evacuated to the nearest C.C.S.; the remainder 9 men unfit to march were carried in the motor omnibus. Stragglers Post consisting of a Lance Corporal were sent on ahead of the Brigade & stationed at points on the route followed the troop at an interval of three hours in charge of Lieut. J.P. Douglas, with orders to clear these posts - & the House ambulances which moved with the ambulance in rear of the Brigade. The other units were informed where the Stragglers' Posts were & the routes	

Army Form C. 2118.

WAR DIARY
or
INTELLIGENCE SUMMARY. FA. No 50. Dec '16 (3)

(Erase heading not required.)

Place	Date	Hour	Summary of Events and Information	Remarks and references to Appendices
BRETEL	14/12/16	(cntd)	and all men who fell out were instructed to make their way to the nearest post. This arrangement worked very well — all stragglers were collected & the motor Ambulances had only one journey to make. 1.O.R. proceeded on leave — Lieut H.R. GRELLET rejoins from 32nd A.S.A. Train. Capt. R.H. LEIGH (S.R.) joins for duty from No 12 General Hospital.	
NOEUX	15/12/16		Left NOEUX 9.15 am arrives HERICOURT 3.30 pm.	
HERICOURT	16/12/16		Left at 9.15 am arrived PESSY-LÈS-PERNES 4.15 pm. Capt. H.N. STAFFORD delivers lunleave.	
PESSY LÈS PERNES	17/12/16		Left 9.15 am arrives NORRENT FONTES 1.30 pm	
NORRENT FONTES	18/12/16		Left 9.30 am arrives CALONNE SUR LA LYS 3 pm. 3 O.R. proceeds on leave	
CALONNE	19/12/16		C Section under Capt. C.J.B WAY marches to VIEILLE CHAPELLE & commence taking over for No 15 Field Ambulance. Another Lieut. J.P. DOUGLAS transferred to this Unit.	
CALONNE	20/12/16		Unit move to VIEILLE CHAPELLE. Took over main Dressing Station at GREEN BARN & ST VAAST and advanced Dressing station at tral-Tilleul	

Army Form C. 2118.

WAR DIARY
or
INTELLIGENCE SUMMARY. 50th A. Dec 1916 (4)

(Erase heading not required.)

Place	Date	Hour	Summary of Events and Information	Remarks and references to Appendices
NEUVE CHAPELLE	21/12/16		3 O.R. proceed on leave.	
Do	22/12/16		ADMS + Co. inspected the two A.D.S.	
Do	23/12/16		Lt. J.D. MERCER detailed to evacuate to England & struck off strength accordingly. Reinforcements joined. Co. inspected ST VAAST A.D.S.	
Do	24/12/16		ADMS & DDMS calls. Lt. S. CHILD detached from 3rd to DDiv. Sanitary Sect. Box Respirator Drill under Capt. H.H. STAFFORD.	
96	25/12/16		6 O.R. proceed on leave. Lt. H.R. GRELLET detailed for temporary duty with 3/1st D Rail Train.	
Do	27/12/16		Capt. M.W. PATERSON Relieves Capt. R.H. LIEGH at Neuve Bain A.D.S.	
Do	28/12/16		5 O.R. proceeded on leave.	
Do	29/12/16		ADMS inspected	
Do	30/12/16		ADMS inspected	
Do	31/12/16		Nothing of note	

WAR DIARY or **INTELLIGENCE SUMMARY.** 56 K.T.A. Dec /16 (5)

Army Form C. 2118.

The u/m N.co's men were awarded the Military Medal on 19.12.1916.

85598 Sergt. WILLIAMS. W.T. (R.Amb)
58155 Sm.   HATTON. T.   (R.Amb)
59489   "   IVES. R.A.   (R.Amb)
44108   "   MOLLOY. F.J.   (R.Amb)

J.D. Nicholls Lt. Col. R.A.M.C.
Commanding 56 KTA

CONFIDENTIAL.

War Diary

of

Lieut. Col. T. B. Nicholls - R.A.M.C.

Commanding 50th Field Ambulance.

from 1st January 1917 to 31st January 1917.

(Volume 18.)

COMMITTEE FOR THE
MEDICAL HISTORY OF THE WAR
Date   13 MAR. 1917

WAR DIARY
or
INTELLIGENCE SUMMARY.
(Erase heading not required.)

Army Form C. 2118.

January 1917

Place	Date	Hour	Summary of Events and Information	Remarks and references to Appendices
NEILLE CHAPELLE			WAR DIARY of Lieut. Col. T.B. NICHOLLS. R.A.M.C. Commanding 50th Field Ambulance	
	1/1/17		Inspection by A.D.M.S. 37th Division. O.B.N. on the extreme.	
"	2/1/17		Inspection by A.D.M.S.	
"	3/1/17		Capt H.N. STAFFORD relieves Capt S. CHILD at ST VAAST A.D.S. 6.O.R proceed on leave	
"	4/1/17		A.D.M.S. calls. L.O.R. reinforcements joined	
"	5/1/17		A.D.M.S. calls. Lt. ALFORD returns from temp. duty with 8th E. LANCS. Regt + took over GREEN BARN A.D.S. from Capt. M.W. PATERSON	
"	6/1/17		Capt. O.J.B. WAY proceeds on 10 days leave. 6.O.R. proceed on leave. Pte BAKER W.H (No 5988 5) absent to be trained in an Infantry Communion. No 35593 Sgt WILLIAMS, W.T. awarded meritorious service medal (London Gazette Date 2/1/17)	
" - " -	8/1/17		Capt R.H. LEIGH & A/Cpl HOLLINGWORTH. W. detailed to proceed to A.O.D Gas School to Shorncliffe	
" - " -	9/1/17		6. O.R proceed on leave	
" - " -	10/1/17		Lieut H.R. GRELLET returns from temp. duty with 37th Divl. Train	

WAR DIARY or INTELLIGENCE SUMMARY

Army Form C. 2118.

50th D.A.   Jan 1917

Place	Date	Hour	Summary of Events and Information	Remarks and references to Appendices
VIEILLE CHAPELLE	10/1/17		Inspection by D.D.M.S. XI Corps.	
-do-	12/1/17		Lt H R GRELLET relieves Capt H.M. STAFFORD at Sr TOOST A.D.S. 6 O.R. proceed on leave	
-do-	13/1/17		Capt. R H LEIGH relieves Lt. Z.R ALFORD at GreenBarn H.Q.S. Lt. ALFORD proceeds to 8th SOMERSET Regt. for permanent duty. Capt. H.M. STAFFORD (S.R.) transferred to H.M. Regular Army (London Gazette 10/1/17)	
-do-	14/1/17		Inspection by G.O.C. 37th D.A.	
-do-	15/1/17		4 O.R. proceed on leave	
-do-	16/1/17		Capt. A.F. ELLIOTT joins from duty from following promotions made on authority of D.G.M.S. (B 1450/246 of 13/1/17)	
			No 37749 Cpl Gordon G. to be A/Sergeant. — M/Sergt. } to Complete Establishment
58255 Cpl IRWIN J.W. — a/Corporal
39149 L/Cpl. WESTON T. — a/Cpl.
38169 L/Cpl. HOLLINGWORTH E. — a/Cpl.
C. proceeds on leave. following promotions made - auth. D.G.M.S. Circular No 13. } to Complete Establishment
No 39920 Pte HITCHINER A tobe Lee Cpl
36666 Pte SHARVÉ E Lee Cpl
Capt.	

Army Form C. 2118.

Instructions regarding War Diaries and Intelligence Summaries are contained in F. S. Regs., Part II. and the Staff Manual respectively. Title pages will be prepared in manuscript.

WAR DIARY
or
INTELLIGENCE SUMMARY.

50 J.A.   Jan '17   (3)

(Erase heading not required.)

Place	Date	Hour	Summary of Events and Information	Remarks and references to Appendices
VIEILLE CHAPELLE	18/1/17		Capt. S. CHILD proceed Tarcow Temp'y M.S. Charge of 53 W. H.H. Group 6 OR proceed on leave	
- Do -	20/1/17		Capt. S. CHILD returns Capt. C/S WAY } review { Capt. R.H. Capt. A.F. ELLIOTT } { Lieut H.R. GRELLET } at the ADS at { GREEN BARN St. HYLST.	
- Do -	22/1/17		5 O.R. proceed on leave.	
- Do -	23/1/17		G.O.C. 3₁ₜ D.R awards military Cross to Capt. C/B WAY (DRO 2158 ?/23/1/17)	
- Do -	24/1/17		6 OR proceed on leave. Bot Respirators tested with Lachrymating gas at	
- Do -	26/1/17		Lt. H.R. GRELLET proceed Estree aux Temp'y M.O. Charge A70 to Rural Divis'n - Adma called	
- Do -	27/1/17		Capt H.N STAFFORD relieves Capt C/S WAY at GREEN BARN H.P.S.	
- Do -	28/1/17		CO returns from leave. Capt. M.W. PATERSON evacuates & I/c unknown CCS (Aimestailes) Capt S. CHILD & Capt R.H. KEIGH Watch buttons lectures on organisation by St.HYLST. XI Cops temp movement	

2353   Wt. W2544/1454   700,000   5/15   D. D. & L.   A.D.S.S./Forms/C. 2118.

Army Form C. 2118.

WAR DIARY
or
INTELLIGENCE SUMMARY.

50 ? A   Jan 17 (4)

(Erase heading not required.)

Instructions regarding War Diaries and Intelligence Summaries are contained in F. S. Regs., Part II. and the Staff Manual respectively. Title pages will be prepared in manuscript.

Place	Date	Hour	Summary of Events and Information	Remarks and references to Appendices
NEULLE CHAPELLE	31/1/17		Cs visited A Buns + no picket AA Ss. OB Neuville St Vaast Command. 50th Feld Intelligence 37th Division	

CONFIDENTIAL.

War Diary

of

Lieut. Col. T. B. Nicholls - R.A.M.C.

Commanding 50th Field Ambulance.

from February 1st 1917. to February 28th 1917.

(Volume 19.)

WAR DIARY or INTELLIGENCE SUMMARY

Army Form C. 2118.

50 F.A.
Feb 1917

Place	Date	Hour	Summary of Events and Information	Remarks and references to Appendices
NEUVE CHAPELLE	1/2/17	—	War Diary of Lieut Col. T.D Meeks lb Roll O, Burma Army 50th Field Ambulance, 37th Division	
— Do —	2/2/17		One N.C.O. two men evacuated (sick) to No 7 C.C.S., 6 O.R. proceeded on leave. Obtained No 9/3/ Rams.	2/-
— Do —	3/2/17		Six new A.M.S. (GREEN BARN & ST PAST) taken over by 56th Field Ambulance. No 39885 Pte BAKER, W.H. interviewed by GOC VIth Corps as to his fitness for a commission. I was present as witness. 1 N.C.O. evacuated (sick) to #2 London C.C.S. Main dressing station handed over to 15th D.H. Unit left at 1.30 p.m arrived CALONNE-SUR-LA-LYS 4 p.m.	OM
CALONNE-SUR-LA-LYS	4/2/17		6 O.R. proceeded on leave	OM
— Do —	5/2/17		Squad Drill. Field Ambulance Drill. Kit inspection	OBE
— Do —	6/2/17		Drill + CO's Parade	
— Do —	7/2/17		Inspection of unit on parade & Horse Part, by the G.O.C. 37th Div. Capt H.N STAFFORD detailed in Temporary medical charge of 13th Bn Rifle Bde.	
— Do —	8/2/17		Pte BAKER W.H. proceeded to England to Cadet School. Lt. H.R GRELLET returns from Temp'y Med'l Charge of 10th Bn Royal Dublins - on man management lecture on the War Loan to troops by Capt G A WAY.	

Army Form C. 2118.

WAR DIARY
or
INTELLIGENCE SUMMARY.   503 A   Feb 17   (2)
(Erase heading not required.)

Place	Date	Hour	Summary of Events and Information	Remarks and references to Appendices
CALONNE-SUR-LA-LYS	10/2/17		Unit left 10.45 am - arrived BETHUNE 2 pm. One man evac. sick	
BETHUNE	11/2/17		Capt. C.J.B. WAY, Lieut SCHILD & Lieut H.R. GRELLET proceeded with C section to take over A.D.S. at - LES BREBIS & M.D.S. at - BRAQUEMONT /- 72nd J.A.	OBE
BETHUNE	12/2/17		Unit left 10 am arrived BRAQUEMONT 12.15 p.m.	
BRAQUEMONT	13/2/17		Inspected A.D.S. at Loos, BREBIS, also Baths & Soup Kitchen & Baths at MAZINGARBE and BRAQUEMONT.	OBE
-do-	14/2/17		Inspected A.D.S. Beaurepaire & Soup Kitchen at MAROC also visited 100 Regt Aid Posts there.	OBE
-do-	15/2/17		A.D.M.S. called	OBE
-do-	16/2/17		Inspection by Asst. Commander of A.D.M.S.	
-do-	19/2/17		Inspection by A.D.M.S. 1st Corps & A.D.M.S.	OBE
-do-	20/2/17		One man evac. L33 CCS sick. All Blankets disinfected by Thresh Dis Army	

Army Form C. 2118.

WAR DIARY
or
INTELLIGENCE SUMMARY.   50 J.A.   Feb '17   (3)
(Erase heading not required.)

Place	Date	Hour	Summary of Events and Information	Remarks and references to Appendices
BARQUEMONT	21/2/17		ADMS called JBS	
-do-	22/2/17		Inspects A.D.S. Beaver Post. JBS	
-do-	23/2/17		ADMS inspects Latrine in Canadian JUMP LINES at Fm BREBIS, attended by Capt. S. CHILD & Q.O.R. See if these have been wired to, so they are suitable for carrying wounded in certain conditions JBS	
-do-	25/2/17		Capt. M.W. PATERSON relieved Capt. S. CHILD at the A.D.S. on man transferred to Transportation Depot. JBS	
-do-	26/2/17		ADMS called. No. 41680 Sgt JONES H.J. transferred to Transportation Dept. Capt. R.H. LEIGH returned from Leave JBS Capt. H.N. STAFFORD relieves him 13th R. Bde.	
-do-	27/2/17		ADMS called	
-do-	28/2/17		ADMS called. Conference at 11 am his office 11 O'C 7.45 O'Brienly M.D.DRAmce Command, 50 Div.	

2353 Wt. W2514/1454 700,000 5/15 D. D. & L. A.D.S.S./Forms/C. 2118.

CONFIDENTIAL.

War Diary

of

Officer Commanding, 50th Field Ambulance.

from 1st March 1917. to 31st March 1917.

(Volume 20).

Army Form C. 2118

WAR DIARY
—or—
INTELLIGENCE-SUMMARY

(Erase heading not required.)

Instructions regarding War Diaries and Intelligence Summaries are contained in F. S. Regs., Part II. and the Staff Manual respectively. Title Pages will be prepared in manuscript.

50th. F.A.   March 1917.   (1)

Place	Date	Hour	Summary of Events and Information	Remarks and references to Appendices
			WAR DIARY of Lieut. Col.T.B.Nicholls - R.A.M.C. - Commanding 50th. Field Ambulance, 37th.Division	
BRAQUEMONT	1/3/17.		A.D.M.S. called - One N.C.O. and 2 men transferred (sick) to No. 7 General Hospital.	Neuilly Wood Row C.
do	2/3/17.		A.D.M.S. called.	
do	3/3/17.		Unit left BRAQUEMONT at 1-30 p.m. arrived BETHUNE 3-45 p.m. - One man transferred (sick) to No.7 General Hospital. - C.O. evacuated (sick) to No. 33 C.C.S.	
BETHUNE	4/3/17.		One man (A.S.C. M.T.) evacuated (sick) to No. 33 C.C.S. - Two men transferred (sick) to No.7 General Hospital. - Unit left BETHUNE at 12 noon arrived L'ECLEME 4 p.m.	
L'ECLEME	5/3/17.		Unit left L'ECLEME at 11-30 a.m. arrived NEDONCHELLE 3-30 p.m.	
NEDONCHELLE	6/3/17.		One N.C.O. transferred (sick) to No. 7 General Hospital. - One man (A.S.C. H.T.) evacuated (sick) to 2/1st. West Riding C.C.S.	
do	8/3/17.		Unit left NEDONCHELLE at 9-30 a.m. arrived VALHUON 12-30 p.m. - One N.C.O. (A.S.C. M.T.) evacuated (sick) to No. 12 Stationary Hospital.	
VALHUON	9/3/17.		Unit left VALHUON at 9-30 a.m. arrived REBREUVIETTE 4-45 p.m.	
REBREUVIETTE	10/3/17		One man evacuated (sick) to No.12 Stationary Hospital - One man evacuated (sick) to No.6 Stationary Hospital.	
do	11/3/17.		One man evacuated (sick) to No. 12 Stationary Hospital.	
do	12/3/17.		3 N.C.O.s and 24 men report to O.C. 37th. C.C.S. AVESNES for temporary duty. - One N.C.O. rejoins unit from 2/1st. West Riding C.C.S. - C.O. rejoins unit from No. 33 C.C.S. - A.D.M.S. called.	
do	13/3/17.		One N.C.O. and 3 men rejoin unit from No. 7 General Hospital - One man (A.S.C. H.T.) joins unit for duty from 37th. Divl. Train.	

1875 Wt. W593/826 1,000,000 4/15 J.B.C. & A. A.D.S.S./Forms/C. 2118.

Army Form C. 2118

WAR DIARY
—or—
INTELLIGENCE-SUMMARY

(Erase heading not required.)

50th. F.A.

March 1917.   (2)

Instructions regarding War Diaries and Intelligence Summaries are contained in F. S. Regs., Part II. and the Staff Manual respectively. Title Pages will be prepared in manuscript.

Place	Date	Hour	Summary of Events and Information	Remarks and references to Appendices
PERREUVILETTE.	14/3/17.		A.D.M.S. and A.A.Q.M.G. called. - One N.C.O. takes over temporary charge of 111th. Brigade Baths, BUIRE-VILLE.	
do.	15/3/17.		Capt. C.J.B.WAY detailed for temporary duty with 49th. Field Ambulance. Following promotions made on Authority of D.G.M.S.:- No. 35637 Corpl. EVANS.T.C. to be A/Sergeant.- Authority B.1450/530) " 35625 " TOWNSLEY.H.A. to be A/Sergeant - " B.1450/529) To complete " 59180 L/Cpl. WATT.J.M. to be A/Corporal - " B.1450/544) Establishment. " 39920 " HITCHINS.A. to be A/Corporal - " B.1450/543) Conference at office of D.D.M.S. VIth. Corps of A.D.sM.S. and Os.C. Field Ambulances.	
do.	16/3/17.		C.O. visits A.D.M.S. - 3 men evacuated (sick) to No. 12 Stationary Hospital. - One N.C.O. and one man rejoins unit from No. 7 General Hospital. - One N.C.O. (A.S.C. M.T.) rejoins unit from No. 12 Stationary Hospital. - Two N.C.O.s rejoin unit from Base. No. 41853 Sergt.E.B.RADFORD attends four days course at Divl. Gas School.	
do.	17/3/17.		Capt. S. CHILD proceeds on leave. - Capt. R.H.LEIGH relieves Capt. C.J.B.WAY, temporary duty at 49th. Field Ambulance - One N.C.O. and 15 men report to O.C. 37th. C.C.S. for temporary duty.	
do.	19/3/17.		One man rejoins unit from No. 12 Stationary Hospital. - Conference of Regl.Medical Officers of 111th. Brigade and M.O.s of H.Q. 50th. Field Ambulance - One N.C.O. detailed for temporary duty at VIth. Corps Rest Station.	
do.	20/3/17.		C.O. attends conference of Divl: Commander.	9 medical notebooks
do.	21/3/17.		Motor Ambulance Drivers shown routes through ARRAS. - C.O. visits trenches at ARRAS.	
do.	22/3/17.		Remainder of "C" Section under Capt. C.J.B.WAY - M.C.- with Lieut. H.R.GRELLET take over VIth. Corps (Subsidiary) Rest Station, BELLAVESNES, from 45th. F.A. 15th. Division. - One man rejoins unit from No. 5 Stationary Hospital - Two men rejoin unit from No. 12 Stationary Hospital.	

Army Form C. 2118

WAR DIARY
or
INTELLIGENCE SUMMARY

(Erase heading not required.)

50th. F.A.

March 1917.   (3)

Instructions regarding War Diaries and Intelligence Summaries are contained in F. S. Regs., Part II. and the Staff Manual respectively. Title Pages will be prepared in manuscript.

Place	Date	Hour	Summary of Events and Information	Remarks and references to Appendices
FIENBRUVILLERS	23/3/17.		Following promotions made on Authority D.G.M.S. Circular No. 13:- No. 33525 Pte. BESANT.F.C. to be Lance Corpl. } To complete " 40081 " WALKER.W.C. to be Lance Corpl. } establishment. Route March from 2 p.m. to 4 p.m.- N.C.O.s to report on ground covered etc:	
do	24/3/17.		One man rejoins unit from No. 12 Stationary Hospital - One man evacuated (sick) to No. 6 Stationary Hospital. - Night manoeuvres, practice in finding way home in dark.	
do	25/3/17.		One man (A.S.C. M.T.) rejoins unit - Conference of Os.C. F.A.s at office of A.D.M.S.	
do	26/3/17.		Demonstration on use of Thomas's Splint attended by Officers' and N.C.O.s'.	
do	27/3/17.		C.O. visits A.D.M.S.	
do	28/3/17.		One man evacuated (sick) to No. 6 Stationary Hospital.	
do	30/3/17.		Conference of A.D.M.S. and Os.C. F.A.s' at office of D.D.M.S. VIth. Corps - Capt. S.CHILD returns from leave - One O.R. proceeds on leave -112 Brigade Operations attended by two Bearer Sub-Divisions of F.A.	
do	31/3/17.		Conference of Regtl: M.O.s' and Os.C. F.A.g' at office of A.D.M.S. - One O.R. detailed for temporary duty with M.O. i/c troops AVESNES - One N.C.O. and 15 men rejoin unit from temporary duty at 37th. C.C.S. There has been a small epidemic of German Measles, which was probably brought away with the unit from BRAQUEMONT, but has now ceased. Total number of cases "Eleven".	

JBNewth   Lieut. Col. R.A.M.C.
Commanding 50th. Field Ambulance.

Appendix I

War Diary of
O.C. 50th Field Ambulance.
April 1917.

Orders by A.D.M.S. 37th Division.

S E C R E T.   COPY. No. 3

MEDICAL ARRANGEMENTS.
37th. DIVISION.
OPERATIONS.   No.27.

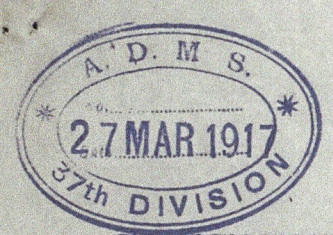

Headquarters,
27 MAR. 1917

The VIth. Corps will attack, on a date to be notified later, with the 3rd, 12th, and 15th. Divisions in the front line and the 37th. Division in Corps Reserve.

The objective of the three leading divisions is the German third line system, from a point about 1,500 yards N.E. of NEUVILLE VITASSE to a point about 500 yards E. of FEUCHY. This objective is denominated the Brown line - the 2 intermediate stages being denominated the Black and Blue line respectively.

The objective of the 37th. Division (Green Line) comprises the village of MONCHY LE PREUX and the neighbouring high land.

By Zero plus 3 hours the 37th. Division will be closed up on the line DAINVILLE, WAGONLIEU, ST.AUBIN, ready to move forward, 112th. Brigade on the right, 63rd. Brigade in the centre and 111th. Brigade on the left.

Here the Brigades will be joined by their Bearer Sub-Divisions.

The Brigades will move forward through ARRAS by the routes shown in the attached map (issued to Field Ambulances only) to the areas of assembly where they will halt and a meal will be taken.

The attack on the Green Line will be carried out by the 112th. and 111th. Brigades, with the 63rd. Brigade in Divisional Reserve.

There are three existing Advanced Dressing Stations which will be used by the 37th. Division - these are shown on the attached map. Of these the right A.D.S. is the better equipped and protected.

From these/

- 2 -

From these Advanced Dressing Stations stretcher cases will be evacuated direct to three Casualty Clearing Stations at AGNEZ-LES-DUISANS by the pooled cars of the 4 Divisions, and those of the 15th. Motor Ambulance Convoy - all under the direction of O.C. 15th. M.A.C.

Walking Wounded will be directed to the Corps Collecting Station, in the Bastion between Porte BAUDIMONT and Porte d'AMIENS, whence they will be evacuated, by wheeled transport, to the Railhead at WARLUS.

As the attack progresses the existing A.D.S.'s may move forward under arrangements made by the 3 leading Divisions.

Field Ambulance will hold two tent Sub-Divisions ready to move forward to form an A.D.S. which it is proposed to locate near the Eastern extremity of FEUCHY.

Field Ambulance will hold a tent Sub-Division ready to move forward to form an A.D.S. which it is proposed to locate at FEUCHY CHAPELLE.

The equipment of these A.D.S.'s will have to be carried by man and pack transport.

The CAMBRAI Road when repaired will probably be too congested for Ambulance transport evacuation but it is hoped that evacuation by the FEUCHY CHAPELLE - FEUCHY road, and thence to ARRAS, will be possible.

Bearer Sub-Divisions attached to Brigades will maintain close touch with the Medical personnel of the Battalions and Os.C. Sub-Divisions will endeavour to keep them in reserve until the Brigades to which they are attached attack, i.e., until the Brown line is passed. O's.C. will also note any suitable position for the establishment of A.D.S.'s in or near the positions indicated above and will send such information to the A.D.M.S. as early as possible.

Lt.Col.D.P.Watson/

- 3 -

LT.COL. D.P.WATSON, R.A.M.C., will co-ordinate the work of all the Bearer Sub-Divisions in action and will establish a report centre at a place to be selected hereafter - he will be supplied with a cycle orderly and, if possible, will be in telephonic communication with A.D.M.S.

The Divisional A.D.S.s at FEUCHY and FEUCHY CHAPELLE will be reinforced as early as possible and the Divisional Field Ambulances will move up to these points as soon as circumstances permit.

Issued at.

10.0 pm

Colonel A.M.S.

A.D.M.S. 37th. Division.

```
Copy No.  1 O.C.48th Field Ambulance.
 "    "   2 O.C.49th Field Ambulance.
 "    "   3 O.C.50th Field Ambulance.
 "    "   4 37th Division "A".
 "    "   5 37th Division "G".
 "    "   6 D.D.M.S. VIth Corps.
 "    "   7 A.D.M.S. 3rd Division.
 "    "   8 A.D.M.S.12th Division.
 "    "   9 A.D.M.S.15th Division.
 "    "  10  63rd Infantry Brigade.
 "    "  11 111th Infantry Brigade.
 "    "  12 112th Infantry Brigade.
 "    "  13 War Diary.
 "    "  14)
 "    "  15)File,
```

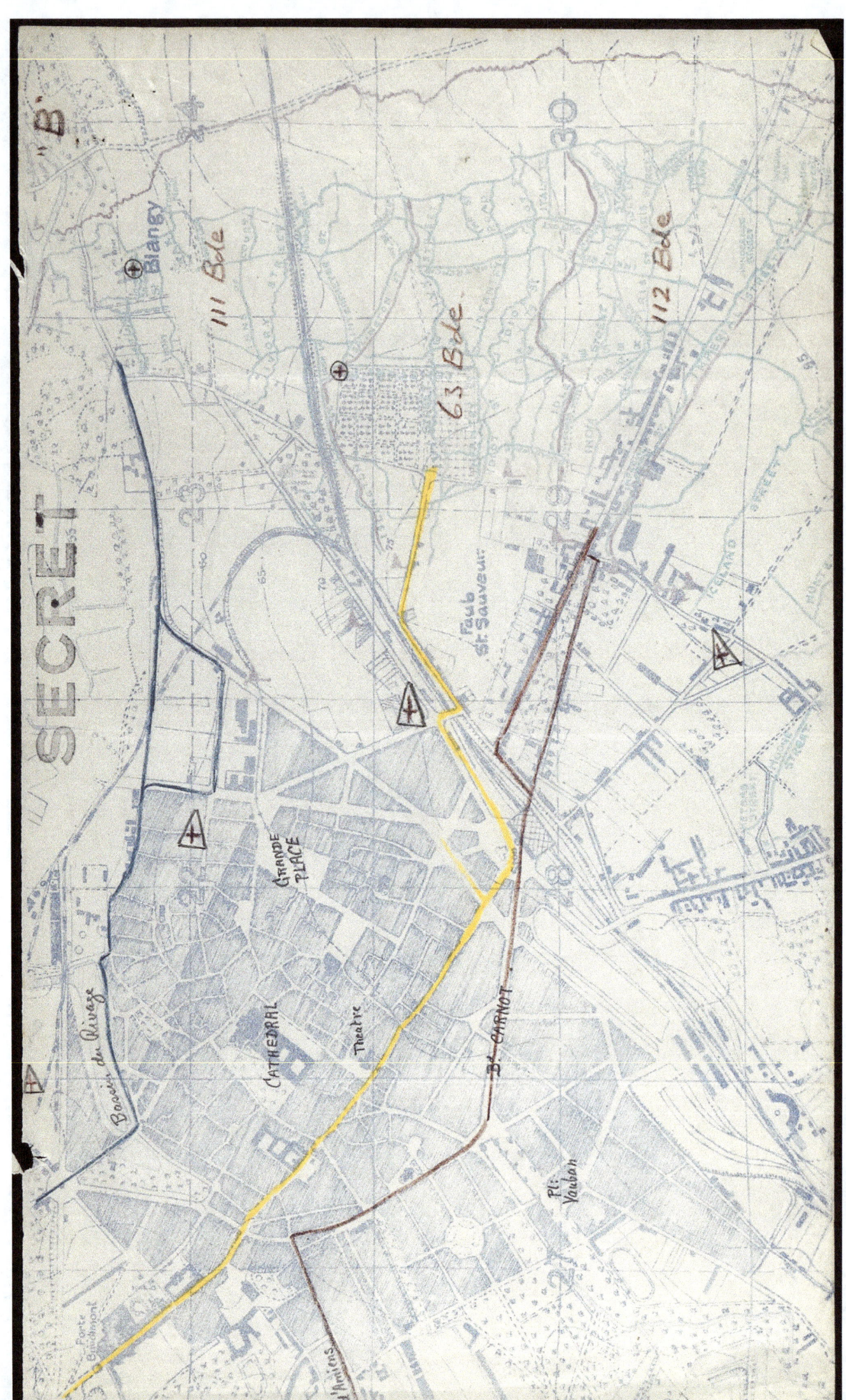

Appendices extracted and attached to 1st Copy of Summary

Confidential

War Diary

of

Officer Commanding, 50th Field Ambulance.

from 1st April 1917.
to 30th April 1917.

(Volume 21.)

COMMITTEE FOR THE
MEDICAL HISTORY OF THE WAR
Date −6 JUN. 1917

Army Form C. 2118.

WAR DIARY
or
INTELLIGENCE SUMMARY.
(Erase heading not required.)

Instructions regarding War Diaries and Intelligence Summaries are contained in F. S. Regs. Part II. and the Staff Manual respectively. Title pages will be prepared in manuscript.

Place	Date	Hour	Summary of Events and Information	Remarks and references to Appendices
Rebreuviette.	1/4/1917.		Commanding Officer judged for Stretcher Bearers competition in 112th Infantry Brigade. Good standard was reached by all. Prize won by 6th Bedfordshire Regiment. One N.C.O. A.S.C.(M.T.) evacuated sick. One N.C.O. R.A.M.C. transferred to Gas School 37th Division, and struck off the strength.	Dhiecele 11.01 Rame Command Soc 977
	2/4/1917.		Administrative conference held by A.A. & Q.M.G. at HOUVIN HOUVIGNEUL at 4 p.m. attended by Captain M.W. Paterson. One N.C.O. and two men detailed for duty under orders of A.D.M.S. as Divisional Clerks at group of C.C.S's at AGNEZ-les-DUISANS. In forthcomming operations these C.C.S's are to play the part of Main Dressing Stations. The necessary particulars are to be extracted by these clerks and sent to A.D.M.S. Office where all returns, statistics, and A. & D. books will be compiled. Instructions of A.D.M.S. 37th Division to accompany Medical arrangements operations No. 27 received (attached in appendix 1.)	OBb
	3/4/1917.		No. 36825 a/sergt H.A.Townsley proceeds to England to Cadet School and is struck of strength accordingly. Captain S. Child relieves Captain C.J.B. Way M.C. at VIth Corps Subsibiary Rest Station, BELLAVESNES /	

Army Form C. 2118.

WAR DIARY
or
INTELLIGENCE SUMMARY.
(Erase heading not required.)

(2)

Instructions regarding War Diaries and Intelligence Summaries are contained in F.S. Regs., Part II. and the Staff Manual respectively. Title pages will be prepared in manuscript.

Place	Date	Hour	Summary of Events and Information	Remarks and references to Appendices
Rebreuviette	3/4/1917.		BELLAVESNES. Operation order No. 28 by A.D.M.S. 37th Division received.	Attached App: 1.
	4/4/1917.		Training of men and Pack Transport animals has been continued each day. Conference of Regimental Medical Officers of 112th Infantry Brigade held at Ambulance H.Qrs. Arrangements to co-ordinate their work with that of the Ambulance were discussed.	
	5/4/1917.		Unit moved to BELLAVESNES, left 8 a.m. arrived 12.30. p.m. marching in rear of 112th Infantry Brigade. Straggler posts were arranged along the various routes and cleared by Motor Ambulances cars after Brigade had passed. Very few fell out. A.D.M.S. called soon after our arrival.	
Bellavesnes	7/4/1917.		B.& C. Sections Bearer Sub-divisions under command of Captain M.W. Paterson moved to WARLUS to follow 112th Infantry Brigade into action. Sergt Major F.H. Leigh with twelve pack animals left to join Captain C.J.B. Way M.C. and Captain R.H. Leigh with twelve pack animals left to join O.C. 49th Field Ambulance who is in charge Divisional Advanced Dressing Stations. Five large Motor Ambulance Cars sent to report to O.C. XVth M.A.C.	
	8/4/1917.		Rev: A.G. Kick C.F. attached this unit, Sergt Major F.C. Herlock (A.S.C.), Sergt Major G.A. Medlock R.A.M.C. with three horsed ambulance wagons, one water cart, two N.C.O's (A.S.C.) and four drivers proceeded to WAGONLIEU to take charge of Horsed Ambulance Wagon Convoy organised by me under orders of D.D.M.S. VIth Corps for evacuation of Walking Wounded from Corps Collecting Station in the BASTION ARRAS to light railway railhead at WARLUS. I visited them at 3 p.m. and all vehicles &c: from other divisions had assembled and were ready to begin. Also visited Captain M.W. Paterson and the bearers of B. & C. Sections who were billetted at WARLUS. Captain H.N. Stafford and Bearer Sub-divisions of A. Section left to report to O.C. 48th Field Ambulance who is in command of Divisional Bearer Company. Eight Animals were sent with two drivers to O.C. 154 Field Coy, R.E. under orders of A.D.M.S.	

This/

Army Form C. 2118.

(3)

WAR DIARY
or
INTELLIGENCE SUMMARY.

(Erase heading not required.)

Instructions regarding War Diaries and Intelligence Summaries are contained in F. S. Regs., Part II. and the Staff Manual respectively. Title pages will be prepared in manuscript.

Place	Date	Hour	Summary of Events and Information	Remarks and references to Appendices
	9/4/1917.		This lending of Ambulance Animals to combatant troops would seem to be a doubtful measure. If the Ambulance has to move during the forthcoming operations, it would be difficult to regain them, and they would be too exhausted to do any work.	
			"Z" Day. Attack commenced at 5.30. a.m. No. 79248 Private F.F. Breakell proceeds to England to Cadet School. Military Medal awarded to No. 37749 Corporal (now A/Sergeant G. Gordon. (Authority 1st Corps No. A 56/256 dated 30/3/1917. Visited WARLUS and found Horsed Ambulance Wagon Convoy running very well.	
	10/4/1917.		Inspection. Horsed Ambulance Wagon Convoy, all satisfactory.	
	11/4/1917.		Rev. A.G. Kick, Sergt Major Horlock, Sergt Major Medlock, transport, and personnel returned from WAGONLIEU. Reports attached, also my original scheme annotated by D.D.M.S. VIth Corps attached. It will be noticed that shelters, trench boards, and refreshments for patients originally suggested but considered unnecessary had to be provided eventually.	App. 2.
	13/4/1917.		Captain M.W. Paterson, Captain H.N. Stafford and Bearers of A,B, & C. Sections returned "no casualties". Report of operations attached.	App. 3
	15/4/1917.		Three Motor Ambulance Cars returned from duty with XV M.A.C. Pack animals, drivers &6: returned from duty with O.C. 49th F.A. and 153 Field Coy. R.E. "no casualties". Animals very fatigued, but no sore backs or injuries. The improvised pack-saddles made after pattern supplied by D.A.&D.O.S. 37th Division, were most unsatisfactory. They were difficult to fit, and not strong enough, all but one broke. Captain A.F. Elliott rejoined from temporary duty with 8th East Lancashire Regiment. He has given me a copy of his report to A.D.M.S. which is of interest, and is therefore attached as appendix IV. It shows that there is still some need of improvement in communications between Bearer Divisions and Regiment. Steps are being taken to train the runners better. Wrote to D.D.M.S. VIth Corps suggesting that the A. & D. Book and A.F. A.36 should be made carbon/	App. IV

Army Form C. 2118.

WAR DIARY
or
INTELLIGENCE SUMMARY.
(Erase heading not required.)

(4)

Instructions regarding War Diaries and Intelligence Summaries are contained in F. S. Regs., Part II. and the Staff Manual respectively. Title pages will be prepared in manuscript.

Place	Date	Hour	Summary of Events and Information	Remarks and references to Appendices
Habarcq	16/4/1917.		Carbon copy, one of the other. This would save a great amount of clerical work and also some errors. I made this suggestion to D.D.G. sometime ago and it met with his approval. Two M.A. Cars detailed for duty with XVth M.A.C. Conference at A.D.M.S. office.	
	17/4/1917.		Unit left BELLAVESNES for HABARCQ. left 2 p.m. arrived 3.15. p.m. Lieut E.M. Brown (T.C.) joined for duty from No. 6 General Hospital, ROUEN. C.O's parade.	
	18/4/1917.		Lieut E.M. Brown detailed for Medical Charge of 37th Divisional Royal Engineers in relief of Captain Marshall. Inspection of Anti Gas appliances.	
	19/4/17.		Lieut E.M. Brown returned to this unit for duty, previous arrangements having been cancelled. One man A.S.C. (H.T.) evacuated sick.	
	20/4/1917.		No. T.4/111468 Sergt Wheatley J. A.S.C.(H.T.) evacuated sick. A.D.M.S. visited. "C" Section under Capt C.J.B.Way M.C. took over A.D.S. at H.13.b.9.2. from 12th Fd.Amb:	
	21/4/1917.		Unit moved to St. Nicholas. Left 11. a.m. arrived 2. 30. p.m. Three clerks rejoined from C.C.S. AGNEZles-DUISANS. Three N.C.O.'s and 23 men rejoined from temporary attachment, 37th C.C.S.	
St Nicholas.	22/4/1917.		Unit moved to the Oil Factory West of St Laurant-Blangy. Ambulance cars sent to Divisional Pool 49th Field Ambulance. One Tent Sub-division under Capt Leight and Lieut Brown sent to A.D.S. at H.13.b.9.2. One N.C.O. and 28 men of 13th North Stafford Regt (Pioneers) arrived to be attached to the unit for digging shelters etc: at the Advanced Dressing Stations.	

Stations/

Army Form C. 2118.

WAR DIARY
or
INTELLIGENCE SUMMARY.
(Erase heading not required.)

Instructions regarding War Diaries and Intelligence Summaries are contained in F. S. Regs, Part II. and the Staff Manual respectively. Title pages will be prepared in manuscript.

Place	Date	Hour	Summary of Events and Information	Remarks and references to Appendices
Laurant-Blangy. St Nicholas.	22/4/17.		Ten of these pioneers sent to Southern Advanced Dressing Station at H.13.b.9.2.	
	"		Bandmaster and 40 other ranks (Divisional Band) attached for duty as Stretcher Bearers.	
	23/4/1917.	8.a.m.	Received orders to get the remaining Tent Sub-division ready.	
		9.20.a.m.	Tent Sub-division and remainder of pioneers ready to move off., Awaiting Col. Roes' party to form Northern A.D.S. at M.S.C.6.6.	
		9.45.a.m.	Tent Sub-division and pioneers marched off.	
		11.15.a.m.	Received orders to send "C" Section into action, and to send Captain M.W. Paterson in relief of Captain Cresswell (wounded), as Medical Officer 13th K.R.R.Corps.	
		12.noon.	"C" Section Bearer Sub-division left under command of Captain Brough 49th Field Ambulance. 129 Casualties dealt with.	
	24/4/1917.	10.a.m.	Divisional Band marched off to A.D.S. C.O. proceeded for duty to Southern A.D.S.	
		3.p.m.	D.D.M.S. XVIth Corps visited A.D.S. 59 Casualties dealt with.	
	25/4/1917.		Capt R.H. Leigh sent from Southern to Northern A.D.S. for duty. Visited Northern A.D.S. Sent 1,000 Sandbags to them. 31 Casualties dealt with.	
	26/4/1917.		Quiet day. Very little shelling. 16 Casualties dealt with.	
	27/4/1917.		Southern A.D.S. heavily shelled by 8inch high velocity gun between the hours of 3 and 5 p.m One shell dropped on the ammunition dump about 20 yards from the A.D.S. The fuses and cartridges exploded, but not the shell. A.D.M.S. and O.C. 49th Field Ambulance were there at the times 22 casualties caused to local troops, mostly gunners – none in personnel. Casualties dealt with 32.	
	28/4/1917.		50 Casualties dealt with.	
	29/4/1917.		Bearer Sub-divisions rejoined at Headquarters. Advanced party from 1st South African Field Ambulance at Southern A.D.S. Short bombardment with gas shells, dropping about 150 yards from the A.D.S. No. casualties. 58 Casualties dealt with.	
	30/4/1917.		A.D.S. handed over to 1st South African Field Ambulance. Ambulance/	

2353 Wt. W2544/1454 700,000 5/15 D.D.&L. A.D.S.S./Forms/C.2118.

Army Form C. 2118.

WAR DIARY
or
INTELLIGENCE SUMMARY.
(Erase heading not required.)

Place	Date	Hour	Summary of Events and Information	Remarks and references to Appendices
	30/4/1917.		Unit moved from St Laurent-Blangy to Ambrines. Personnel by Motor Bus from Rond Point ARRAS. Transport by road.	
			There has not been sufficient time to collate reports from the bearer sub-divisions and the advanced Dressing Stations. These will be sent as an appendix to next months diary.	
			Roll of casualties sustained during recent operations.	
			No.37294 Capt Stafford H.N. Wounded.	
			" 35593 Sergeant Singleton H. Missing	
			" 77644 Private Williams W.T. Wounded	
			" 103810 " Jenkins W. " No. 41867 Pte Rhodes W. Killed.	
			" 37348 " Price J.W.D. " " 88063 " Pitt S.E. "	
			" 35591 " Hill H. " " 37461 " Hart W.H. "	
			" 40881 " O'Dea J. " " 38967 " Tatum H. "	
			" 39933 " Watson A.W. " " 35590 " Seville J.B. "	
			" 37799 " Knowles B.C. " " 88062 " Parker L.C. "	
			" 38184 " Stewart R.J. "	
			" 33990 " Johnson S.J. "	
			" 36028 " Stringer A. "	
			" 38079 " Weddle J.W. "	
			" 35589 " Knowles R.H. Gassed (Shell)	
			" 49993 " Smalley H.H. Wounded	
			" 94507 " Baines J.A. "	
			Lewis G.F. "	
			JBNewallo.	
			Lt Col R.A.,M.C.	
			Commanding 50th Field Ambulance.	

SECRET.

INSTRUCTIONS TO ACCOMPANY MEDICAL ARRANGEMENTS

OPERATIONS   No. 27.

On the first day of bombardment patients in Field Ambulances will be evacuated. This does not apply to cases likely to recover in a week in Corps Rest Stations. Itch cases (except very severe ones) will be discharged to duty.

During active operations wounded of VI Corps will be evacuated as follows:-

Sitting and Lying cases to C.C.S's at AGNEZ-LEZ-DUISANS.

Walking cases (by metre guage railway) to No. 6 Stationary Hospital FREVENT or (by road) to No. 37 C.C.S. AVESNES.

Self-inflicted wounds to No. 37 C.C.B. AVESNES.

The number of sick evacuated to C.C.S's should be reduced to a minimum. They should be, as far as possible, retained in Rest Stations. This also applies to men suffering from slight wounds who will be fit to rejoin their units in a few days.

Each C.C.S. and Main Dressing Station will form a dump of stretchers and blankets where ambulance cars can obtain the necessary number of these articles to complete.

All cases treated in Dressing Station, who, in the opinion of the M.O. will not require further treatment at the C.C.S. will have the letter "O" marked conspicuously on the envelope of the Medical Card. The M.O. at the C.C.S. will use his own discretion as to whether such cases do, or do not, require further treatment.

Eye, Ear and Dental cases are not to be sent for treatment unless urgent.

On receipt of orders each Field Ambulance will detail five large Ambulance Cars to report at Headquarters of 15th Motor Ambulance Convoy on the LOUEZ road at L.9.b.7.3. Each driver to be provided with three days rations.

Os.C. A.D.S's, will detail special orderlies to all cars containing patients requiring special attention. These orderlies will report to O.C., M.A.C. at the controlling station so that they may be returned to their units as early as possible.

All papers are to be taken from wounded prisoners of war at dressing stations and sent with them to C.C.S's.

Particulars of officers and other ranks who die (or are brought in dead) at A.D.S's or while under charge of Field Ambulance personnel, are to be sent to A.D.M.S. as early as possible.

The following order is to be re-published in the orders of Field Ambulances and read out on 3 consecutive parades:-

"Property found on a deceased officer or man or which has
"been found on the Field of Battle, it to be considered to
"be property in the custody of the Government. It must be
"dealt with in accordance with G.R.O. 1387 and 549.
"Looting on the battle field is one of the most serious of
"Military offences. The maximum penalty is to suffer death
"by being shot. In future no case will be leniently dealt
"with".

Special care is to be exercised in the examination of all letters and parcels before despatch from unit to the Field Post Office.

All R.A.M.C. battle casualties are to be reported as early as possible to the A.D.M.S.

2nd Lieut. BROMAGE, 13th Bn. Rifle Brigade has been appointed Divisional Burial Officer.

2nd Lieut. WILLIAMS, 4th Middlesex Regt is Divisional Dumps Officer.

The iron ration normally carried is designated the "Emergency Iron Ration".

In addition to this one iron ration is to be carried by all ranks who are intended to pass through ARRAS on Z Day. Men will therefore be fully rationed up to Z day plus 1 day inclusive on entering ARRAS without counting the emergency ration.

Two additional iron rations per man have been dumped at a Divisional Dump on BLANGY road.(G.23.a.3.2) - these will be drawn on nights of Z and Z plus 1 days for consumption on Z plus 2 and Z plus 3 days respectively.

3 days oats rations must be carried for every animal which is intended to go through ARRAS with the exception of pack animals (which will carry only the unexpended portion

of the days ration) as three days oat ration for these is now dumped at G.23.a.3.2. and hay will also be dumped here for pack animals.

The town water supply of ARRAS will be piped forward along the CAMBRAI Road as rapidly as possible.

Nothing is to be carried on water carts in addition to the vehicles equipment except empty petrol tins and oats for the animals.

Soda tablets for sterilizing water will be issued at the refilling point on "Y" day to all units - 500 to each Field Ambulance.

Salvage - Great assistance can be given to salvage work if every one will pick up and bring some article to the nearest battlefield salvage dump.

On the night of Y/Z days two thirds of the Division will be in tents or bivouac shelters. All Field Ambulance tents which are to be put up in the forward area must be thoroughly camouflaged. Kutch should be demanded from Ordnance. No white tents may be pitched in the forward area.

All units must have got rid of surplus baggage by noon of 4th April, after which nothing further can be received at the Divisional Store at ROELLECOURT.

Col. A. M. S.
A. D. M. S. 37th Divn.

2 - AVR 1917

SECRET.   Copy No.......

R.A.M.C. 37th DIVISION.

OPERATION ORDER.   No. 28.
SUPPLEMENTARY TO ORDER No. 27.

Headquarters,
3rd April, 1917.

1. During the forthcoming operations the whole of the Bearer Sub-divisions will be under the command of Lt. Col. D.P. WATSON, R.A.M.C., who will be designated O.C. Bearer Company.

The three A sub-divisions forming his first and the Band and Barn Owls his second reserve.

The A.D.M.S. is to be kept informed of the movement of these reserves.

2. A forward dump of Medical material is being formed at G.23.c.1.9. East of ARRAS. The mule convoy (36 mules) will re-load here after taking up their first load to the Divisional A.D.S's.

3. The Head Quarters of 50th Field Ambulance will be at BELLAVESNES, those of 48th and 49th Field Ambulances will be at DUISANS under Lt. Col. W.F. ROE, D.S.O., R.A.M.C. - he will have the quartermasters of the two units at his disposal and three reserve/ tent sub-divisions and he will control the forward dump of medical material and the reserve dump which will be formed at his headquarters.

4. Lt. Col. ROE, will be prepared to move the headquarters of the 48th and 49th Field Ambulances forward to the positions of the Divisional A.D.S's when wheeled traffic to these becomes practicable.

5. Lt. Col. T.B. NICHOLLS, R.A.M.C., will control the evacuation of walking wounded from the Bastion to WARLUS and will be in command of the branch of the VIth Corps Rest Station at BELLAVESNES. He will be prepared to move forward on receipt of orders from the A.D.M.S. and must be ready to obtain instructions, in direct communication with D.D.M.S. if necessary, as to disposal of patients and stores at BELLAVESNES and the return to his unit of personnel at Casualty Clearing Stations etc.

6. The Field Ambulance motor cyclists will be disposed of as under on Y day :-

(2).

1 Cyclist from 48th Field Ambce to A.D.M.S. Office.
1   "   " 48th   "   "   to the C.C.S's at AGNEZ LES DUISANS for Divisional duty ∅.
1   "   " 49th   "   "   to 19 C.C.S. for Corps duty.
1   "   " 49th   "   "   to Headquarters of unit.
1   "   " 50th   "   "   to Headquarters of unit.
1   "   " 50th   "   "   to Bastion ∅.
∅ To carry W.3210 &c, to A.D.M.S. Office.

7. Runners will be provided with red bands 1½ inches wide round the left forearm - the following runners will be detailed - one to each O.C. a bearer sub-division by the Field Ambulance concerned - O.C. Bearer Company will detail one R.A.M.C. runner for himself and one, from his second reserve, to report at Divisional Report Centre at Zero plus 8 hours.

The A.D.M.S's runners will be Ptes Cunnington and Harrison, R.A.M.C.

8. The office of A.D.M.S. will be at AGNEZ-LES-DUISANS near the cemetery S. of that village - all ordinary office work and the statistical work of the three Field Ambulances will be conducted here.

The Divisional Report Centre will remain at AGNEZ-LES-DUISANS until the order to move through ARRAS has been given when it will move to G.29.a.1.1. ("HORSE SHOE CAVE").

The A.D.M.S. will be at Divisional Report Centre, the D.A.D.M.S. at AGNEZ-LES-DUISANS.

Captain R.A.M.C.
for Colonel A.M.S.
A.D.M.S. 37th Division.

Issued at
12 noon

Copy No. 1 O.C. 48th Field Ambulance.
 "   "   2 O.C. 49th Field Ambulance.
 "   "   3 O.C. 50th Field Ambulance.
 "   "   4 D.D.M.S. VIth Corps.
 "   "   5 37th Division "A".
 "   "   6 37th Division "G".
 "   "   7 File.
 "   "   8 War Diary.

Appendix II

WAR DIARY of
O.C. 50th Field Ambulance
    April 1917.

Report on Evacuation of Walking Wounded from
The BASTION - ARRAS to WARLUS.

Secret

Bridge over fosse
from Bastion.

1. A.D.S. positions in
German 3rd line, 12th & 15th
Div: areas. 2.

A.D.M.S. 37th Div
Please thank Lt. Col. Nicholls for
the trouble he has taken in this
matter. I have had it carefully
put in notes. Cars are almost
certain to be available for the 2nd
half of journey. 12 horse ambulances
2nd suffice for the 1st half, if not
more will be put on. This work
may not be necessary the 1st day.

P.T.O

III

O.C
50th F. Ambulance

For information

C.W. Treherne
for Captain
Col. A.M.S.
2 - AVR 1917   A.D.M.S. 37th Divn.

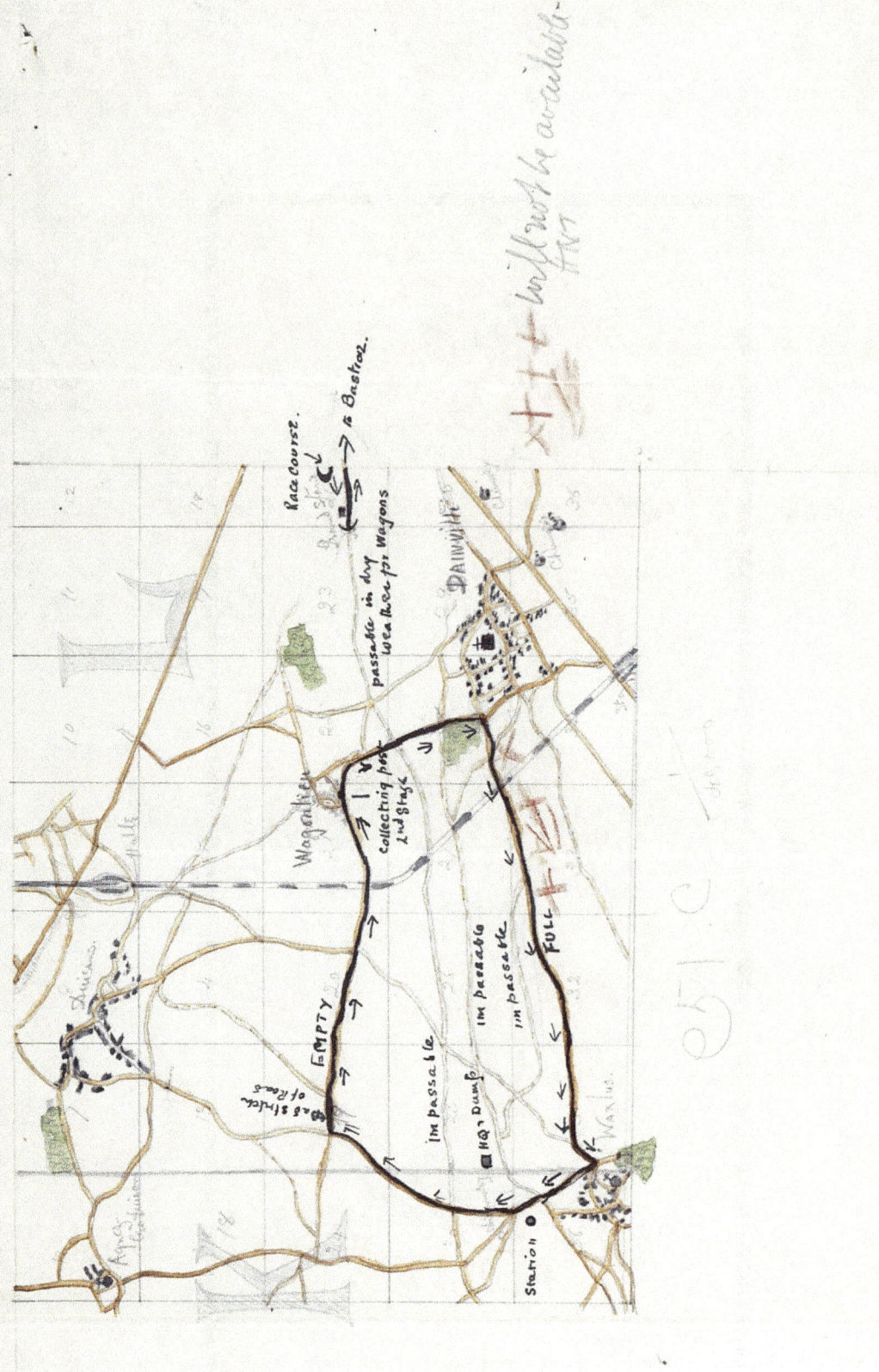

SCHEME FOR EVACUATION OF WALKING WOUNDED.

1. Headquarters, Horse Lines, Ration and Forage Dump, near WARLUS Station.
   2 G.S. Waggons will be required to draw rations and forage.

2. **SPARE ANIMALS**
   will be required at rate of pair per six pairs to replace casualties and exhausted animals.
   First stage of journey is past a large number of guns and is under shell fire.
   The Road from the BASTION to the RACECOURSE has been recently registered by hostile artillery.

3. **PERSONNEL.**
   2 Cooks.
   3 Farriers - with Maltese Cart and Forage. *Forage to be dumped either at Race Course or Wagonlieu*
   2 R.A.M.C. Sergt.-Majors to superintend loading at WAGONLIEU (1 as relief) and to give First Aid if necessary.
   2 Stretcher Squads on track where wounded walk in case of shelling or men becoming exhausted. *Should be handy.*
   2 men for Soup Kitchen at WAGONLIEU.
   9 A.S.C. N.C.O.s - 4 and 4 as reliefs, to superintend the convoy - one i/c Waggon and Horse Lines.
   1 man for Sanitary Duties. *Already one at Bastion, & one at Warlus.*
   1 Despatch Rider. *I do not propose any further buffets.*
   2 men for Soup Kitchen at WARLUS.

4. **TIME TAKEN**
   1st. Stage - about 1½ miles - ½ hour each way. If dry weather and track is used to WAGONLIEU - 1 hour each way.
   2nd. Stage - 3 hours. *1 hour each way. Will most probably be by Car however.*
   Empty Stage - about 4 miles - 1¼ hours.
   Full Stage - about 4 miles - 1¾ hours, as this follows lorry route and delays will occur.
   Allowing for Breakdowns and delays, this convoy working 12 vehicles at a time, will only evacuate 720 casualties in 10 hours work, and this will decrease after the first day, as animals become tired.
   As heavier casualties are expected, more waggons will be necessary.
   Patients should be sent out of BASTION in batches of 12 at 10 minutes' interval to avoid having waggons waiting near gun positions. *yes.*
   Suggested that each Field Ambulance in Corps supplies at least
   1 G.S. Waggon in addition to 2 for supplies - 14 in all. *Rations to be dumped for own horses.*
   Extemporised covers and seats should be provided for G.S. Waggons.
   Do not propose to use them for patients.

5. **SHELTER.**
   There is no shelter for patients either at WARLUS or WAGONLIEU.
   Tents should be provided. *Marquees & buffets will be provided.*
   Tentage required:-
   WAGONLIEU
   3 Operating Tents for patients.
   1 Bell Tent for Aid Post and Soup Kitchen personnel. *Not required.*
   WARLUS
   12 Operating Tents for patients (number depends on frequency of trains).
   1 Operating Tent for Rations and Forage.
   4 Bell Tents for Personnel.
   1 for M.O. at Entraining Centre.

6. **RATIONS**
   Rations and Forage to be drawn from 50th. F.A. at BELLAVICHES after third day. *Other arrangements probable after 1st or at any rate 2nd day.*
   Water available only at WARLUS.
   2 Water Carts required. *Provided at Warlus buffet.*
   Vehicles should be equipped with Empty Petrol Tins for watering animals.

7. **EQUIPMENT.**
   8 Camp Kettles. *What for? Cooking for drivers and orderlies only required.*

continued/

7. EQUIPMENT (continued).
   2 Soyer's Stoves for Soup Kitchens.
   1 case Butcher's Implements.
   12 Hurricane Lamps.
   72 Drinking Mugs.
   1 Surgical Haversack.
   1 set Farrier's Equipment complete.

   [handwritten: Entraining station provided. Only vehicles for carrying required.]
   [handwritten: probably not required, shown by...]

8. ROADS.
   Routes shown on attached sketch map - chosen in conjunction with A.P.M. 3rd. Division and conform to Traffic Circuits. Other roads shown between are only mud tracks unmetalled.
   Track from RACECOURSE To WAGONLIEU is very heavy going in wet weather. Trench Boards should be provided if possible. Could *[handwritten: not possible]* be used by Horse Transport in dry weather. All roads excepting DAINVILLE - WARLUS are bad and as Ambulance Waggons are very heavy in draught, some animals will become exhausted - spares as detailed in (2) are absolutely necessary. *[handwritten: yes]*
   [handwritten left margin: not available]
   Road in square 19 central (51c- 1/40000) is bad and will need repairing - metal is available and repairs can be done by spare drivers.
   [handwritten left margin: where is this road]
   Road from WAGONLIEU to DAINVILLE is closed to Traffic. A.P.M. 3rd. Division states that application to the Corps must be made to open it.
   [handwritten: Cannot be used as Dainville - Warlus route will not be available]

[signature: J.B. Nicholls]

In the Field.   Lieut.Col. R.A.M.C.
27/3/17.   Commanding 50th. Field Ambulance.

Report on evacuation of walking wounded from BASTION ARRAS
to WARLUS by Horse Ambulances.

Sir,

I beg to report for your information that I concentrated 12 Horse Ambulances at WAGONLIEU between 9 a.m. to 9.30. a.m. on the 8th inst from the following divisions.

3rd Division 1 each from No's 7. 8. and 142 Fd.Ambulances.
12th   "   1 each from No's 36. 37. and 38   do.
15th   "   3 from 45th Field Ambulance.
37th   "   3 from 50th Field Ambulance.

I established the Horse and Wagon Lines at WAGONLIEU and detailed the N.C.O's to their various duties. I sent a Sergeant to report to O.C. Collecting Station, BASTION to ascertain the time the Horse Ambulances would be required. I also received orders from the O.C. Collecting Station BASTION that all walking wounded had to be loaded on the field behind the BASTION, contrary to the arrangements made by you previously.

The first batch of wounded came out of the BASTION at 8 a.m. Two Sergeants and six Ambulances were detailed for the first relief, but this was found to be insufficient, so I at once detailed three additional Ambulances, and sent a message to you to this effect.

Additional 12 Ambulances reported between 2 p.m. and 4 p.m. I arranged these into reliefs which worked with *out a* hitch.

At 8.45. a.m. Sergeant Knell 50th Field Ambulance reported that 3 Ambulances had been directed by a Staff Officer to go nearer into ARRAS on their second journey but were found and brought back by this N.C.O. This did not interfere with the evacuation as there were no cases waiting removal.

At 4 p.m. 10th inst I despatched 9 Ambulances to do duty between THOMPSONS CAVE Sheet 51.b.G 29.c. and TILLOY under 2 Sergeants (one 45th F.A. and one of 46th F.A.) I gave the senior N.C.O. instructions to report to the A.D.M.S. Office

Advanced Report Centre, G 29.a.1.1. under your instructions.
At 12.50. p.m. 10th inst I received Orders from D.D.M.S. that all cases were to go to C.C.S. at AGNES-le-DUISANS until further orders, this was arranged and carried out accordingly.
At 10. a.m. 11th inst I received orders from you to despatch all Ambulances back to their various divisions, these were despatched by 1 p.m. as several horses required little rest. All horses were watered and fed at regular intervals also rested properly, they all worked well and returned in good condition to their units.

Private Wright R.A.M.C. No. 8 Field Ambulance had his leg broken while attending a patient on the ~~seed~~ back foot board, by the pole of an ambulance in rear which was caught in a shell hole. He was sent to C.C.S. I reported the case to the O.C. at the BASTION.

Everything worked very smoothly, and good arrangements were made to guide the patients along the track after dark both by improvised lamps and guides.

12/4/17.
In the Field.

Sharlock S.S.M.
A.S.C. attd: 50th Fd. Ambulance
i/c Horse Ambulance Convoy.

BASTION - WAGONLIEU - WARLUS route for walking wounded
April 9th and 10th 1917.

9th. Morning and afternoon numbers not in excess of Motor Ambulance accommodation from about 9 p.m. to 4 a.m. number of wounded arriving at WAGONLIEU considerably more than Motor Ambulances could get away. Met situation by getting the more fit to walk on toward WARLUS hoping that Motor Ambulances working on WARLUS side of the "bad patch" would not be so overtaxed.

Cold intense and no shelter whilst waiting. Hd.Qrs R.G.A. (WAGONLIEU) kindly erected one bell tent and one shelter which proved extremely useful.

Two cases arrived in state of collapse having to be carried, fainted on reaching tent, revived on receiving brandy and sal-volatile. About 7 p.m. Colonel Humphrey (O.C. 37th Divisional Train) sent to WAGONLIEU his canteen van and three orderlies with a good supply of coffee, biscuits, and cigarettes. Every man received hot coffee and one packet each of biscuits and cigarettes, this was an invaluable adjunct considering the weather and the waiting.

Lieut Sheppard (Traffic Control)(WAGONLIEU) rendered valuable assistance in personally guiding parties on WARLUS Road. He also sent four men to act as guides on Grand Stand - (WAGONLIEU) route.

10th. 6 a.m. Two of Y.M.C.A. staff came from DAINVILLE and relieved the three A.S.C. orderlies at the coffee stall and remained till evening. Numbers of wounded greatly diminished from about 4 a.m. all cases taken on by car after that hour.

Albert G. Kick C.F.
attd: 50th Field Ambulance.

Copy.

C/1046/6.

Secret.

To,
   O.C.,
      50th Field Ambulance.

      I have arranged with D.D.M.S. to place five cars at your disposal at WARLUS at "ZERO". All cars are reporting to me on the evening of "X" day, so yours will be detailed for that duty at my Headquarters.

      (Signed) Cyril Helen.

3/4/17,
In the Field.
      Capt R.A.M.C.
      Commdg 15th Motor Ambulance Convoy.

To,
   W.O.
      i/c Transport Walking Wounded,
         WAGONLIEU.

      No further caes are to be sent to WARLUS railhead until further orders. Convoy cars are to convey them to C.C.S. at AGNES-les-DUISANS. A.F. 3210 will accompany the men.

      (Signed) H.N. Thompson,
         Colonel,

12.50. p.m.
10/4/17,
In the Field.
      D.D.M.S. VI Corps.

To,
    O.C.,
        50th Field Ambulance.

Please arrange to send nine Ambulances (Wagon) with two days rations for duty between THOMPSONS CAVE Sheet 51.b. g.29.c. and TILLOY where an A.D.S. is being formed, if possible 3 from each Division, 3rd, 12th, and 15th.

N.C.O. to report at A.D.M.S. Office Advanced Report Centre g.29.a.1.1.

This is under authority of D.D.M.S. Vl Corps.

If you are unable to send so many on account of fatigue of horses let me know number sent.

I understand that the Horse Ambulance service between BASTION and WARLUS is being supplemented by M.A.C. Cars.

(Signed) C.W. Treherne,

Capt R.A.M.C.
D.A.D.M.S.
for Col: A.M.S.
A.D.M.S., 37th Division.

In the Field.

(Note)

Nine Ambulances sent under two Sergeants one of 45th F.A. and one of 46th F.A.

Two Ambulances One 37th F.A. and one 38th F.A.

Three   "   45th Field Ambulance.

Three   "   One No. 7 F.A. One No. 8 F.A. and one No.142 F.A.

Copy of Wire.

To,
    O.C.,
        50th Field Ambulance.

Senders No: M.S. 205. 10/4/17.

Send horsed ambulance back to Divisions to-morrow. A.A.A.
            From:- D.D.M.S. Vlth Corps

Appendix. IV

War diary of
O.C. 50th Field Ambulance.
April 1917.

Report by M.O. i/c 8th E. Lancs. Regt.

Report on 8th East Lancs Regimental Aid Post
during recent operations.

To,
    A.D.M.S.,
        37th Division.

From,
    M.O.
        i/c 8th East Lancs Regiment.

Sir,

April 9th. Aid Post marched with Battalion to West of ARRAS later advanced with regiment to old British Front line, and thence to German second line trenches, up to this point the battalion suffered only two casualties. From here Aid Post advanced with Battalion which eventually occupied a line west of enemy third line system. During this advance, we for the first time came under machine gun fire and several casualties occurred. My bearer squad from 50th Field Ambulance was sent back to A.D.S. with one case. Aid Post eventually established in a shell hole about 60 yards behind battalion front, and runner sent back to inform A.D.S. of our position. We remained here during the night, and received several casualties from battalion. We were rejoined by bearer squad and runner.

April 10th. The enemy line having been taken Aid Post advanced from Fenchy Chapelle with the battalion to a line from Les Fosses Farm northwards towards Monchy, during the advance we suffered casualties from shell fire and bearer squad carried back one stretcher case. Aid Post was established in cellar in Les Fosses Farm in front line and A.D.S. informed of our position. During night a number of wounded including eight stretcher cases were treated.

April 11th. Sent to A.D.S. for squads, and a Thomas' splint for fractured thigh. Three squads arrived with splint and three cases sent back.

During the day a number of wounded, mostly walking cases were treated in three cellars and a barn and stable until the latter were destroyed by enemy shell fire. I was able to get a stove going in one cellar and supply hot tea and iron rations to the cases which could not walk. during the day I sent four notes to A.D.S. One to Brigade and one to A.D.M.S, asking for two stretcher parties, to none of which I received any reply. About 5 p.m. a carrying party from East Lancs Regt, brought up three stretchers and took back three of my cases. About 10 p.m. having a number of wounded cavalry men, I got into communication with the cavalry Ambulance, who sent up a large squad and cleared my Aid Post of twenty four stretcher cases in two journeys.

Battalion was then relieved and I handed over Aid Post to M.O. of Middlesex Battalion.

The last stretcher squads I obtained from infantry Ambulance came at 6 a.m. After this, in spite of several messages, which were apparently never received, I could not obtain stretcher squads. Fortunately I was able to keep my cases warm, and feed them in the cellars, I should, probably, have had deaths from exposure, owing to the adverse weather conditions, as several of my cases were not moved until twelve hours after I had received them.

I have the honour to be sir,
Your obedient servant,

[signature] Capt R.A.M.C.

14/4/17,
In the Field.

M.O. i/c 8th East Lancs Regiment.

Appendix V.

War diary of
O.C. 50th Field Ambulance.
April 1917

Suggested alterations in ~~existing~~ organisation

Alterations in Medical arrangements suggested by operators commencing 9th April 1917.

1. A.D.S.
   a. ORGANISATION.

   The senior M.O. should, unless there is very heavy work on occupy himself entirely with organisation, admissions, evacuation and chosing those cases which need attention first.

   Officers were not sufficiently informed of what was contemplated and thus could display little initiative. They did not appear to have been detailed for any particular duties, nor where they informed of what equipment was taken. Another difficulty arose from the fact that the Officers, N.C.O's and men were strange to each other and had not been trained together.

   An officer should go forward with the Bearer sub-divisions to reconnoitre. Much time could then be saved in pushing up the A.D.S.

   Bearer Sub-divisions should not have their H.Q. at the A.D.S., it leads to overcrowding and confusion.

   b. EQUIPMENT.

   Picks and shovels are essential, two axes felling would be useful, as also three sandbags per man as carried by the infantry.

   Rubber gloves should be used, it is much easier to keep them clean than one's hands with the small amount of water available.

   A scale of equipment to be taken up by the mule convoy should be drawn up and circulated for information of all.

   Four Wagon covers with rope, hammer and nails for making extemporised shelter for wounded.

   Bleaching powder should be carried with water tins.

THE UTILIZATION OF HEAT OF INCINERATORS,
by Capt.(Actg.Lt.Col.) T.B. Nicholls.
ROYAL ARMY MEDICAL CORPS.

One of the greatest obstacles to Preventive Medicine in a Division is the difficulty of keeping the troops clean, the main reason being the question of obtaining and transporting sufficient fuel.

On one occasion coal was almost impossible to obtain, when on thinking over alternative sources of heat, the Incinerator suggested itself.

The amount of heat in a brick built Incinerator is so great as to fuse a glass bottle and usually this heat is allowed to go to waste.

The first attempt to utilize it, was the placing of the tank of a derelict water cart on the top of the incinerator; but, while this supplied enough hot water for hospital purposes, it was not sufficiently rapid in its action.

An improvement was effected by constructing a Thermo-Syphon on the principle of the ordinary hot water supply of a dwelling-house.

This consists of a small boiler, made from an oil-drum, in the centre of the fire of the Incinerator with an inlet and an outlet pipe forming the syphon, and a 100 gallon tank as a reservoir.

The arrangement is shown as Fig.1.

A system of this description will consume a G.S. Wagon load of refuse per diem, and will provide enough hot water to bath about 300 men at the rate of 60 per hour, if connected to a group of five roses, as shewn in the right half of Fig.2.

Attention was then directed to making use of the waste heat from the chimney, and the prevention of undue loss of heat from the tank.

A shed was built on to the nack wall of the Incinerator for use as a dryingroom.

The chimney was prolonged, and led through the shed, and the hot water tank placed inside as in the left half of fig.2.

This arrangement worked admirably, and it is proposed to adapt it for use in a laundry.

In this case the whole plant would be larger, and it would be necessary to utilise the refuse of a larger area to provide the fuel.

It would seem that the success of this attempt warrants a more extended trial, and, if found sucessful, would result in the saving of a very large amount of coal.

The details of construction are shewn in the accompanying diagrammatic sketches, which are not drawn to scale.

29/7/1917,
In the Field.

CONFIDENTIAL.

War Diary

of

Officer Commanding, 50th Field Ambulance

From 1st May 1917. to 31st May 1917.

(Volume 22)

Army Form C. 2118.

WAR DIARY
or
INTELLIGENCE SUMMARY

(Erase heading not required.)

Instructions regarding War Diaries and Intelligence Summaries are contained in F.S. Regs., Part II. and the Staff Manual respectively. Title pages will be prepared in manuscript.

Place	Date	Hour	Summary of Events and Information	Remarks and references to Appendices
AMBRINES.	1/5/17.		Capt. J.P. Lowson. R.A.M.C., T.C. joined for duty. One N.C.O. A.S.C. and one other rank R.A.M.C. rejoined from hospital.	Lieut.Col. R.A.M.C. Comdg. 50th Field Ambulance.
	2/5/17.		One N.C.O. evacuated sick, one man rejoined unit from hospital. Thirty-four other ranks detailed for temporary duty at 19 C.C.S.	
	3/5/17.		Inspection by A.D.M.S.	
	4/5/17.		Lieut. W.G. McCONNELL. R.A.M.C. (T.C.) posted to unit for duty from 49th Field Ambulance. This officer on joining division was immediately sent with detachment to 37th C.C.S. and I have not yet seen him.	
	5/5/17.		A.D.M.S. visited. Capt. A.F. Elliott. R.A.M.C. (T.C.) posted to A.D.M.S. ABBEVILLE for duty and is struck off strength accordingly. One man rejoined from temporary duty with M.O. i/c Troops AVESNES-le-COMTE.	
	7/5/17.		Thirty-four other ranks rejoined from temporary duty at 19.C.C.S.	
	8/5/17.		A.D.M.S. visited. One N.C.O. A.S.C. evacuated sick.	
	9/5/17.		Transport Competition between the three Field Ambulances of the Division. Three G.S. wagons packed, one limbered wagon, two water carts, two horsed ambulanced wagons shewn. This unit won by 100 marks.	
	10/5/17.		Route march with 112th Brigade. Conference at A.D.M.S.'s office.	
	11/5/17.		Capt. M.W. Paterson. rejoins from temporary medical charge of 13th Batt. K.R.R.C.	
	13/5/17.		Competition for best turned out officers' chargers in the division. Capt. Child's charger took 6th place in under 15 hands class.	

Army Form C. 2118.

WAR DIARY
or
INTELLIGENCE SUMMARY
(Erase heading not required.)

Instructions regarding War Diaries and Intelligence Summaries are contained in F. S. Regs., Part II. and the Staff Manual respectively. Title pages will be prepared in manuscript.

Place	Date	Hour	Summary of Events and Information	Remarks and references to Appendices
AMBRINES.	14/5/17.		Field day with 112th/Brigade. Unit exercised in forming and moving Advanced dressing stations Bearer sub-division work and the improvement of communications	
	16/5/17.		Capt.J.P.Lowson. transferred to No.6.Stationary Hospital for duty. One man evacuated sick.	
	17/5/17.		One man evacuated sick.	
	18/5/17.		Unit moved to GOUVES left 11-30am. arrived 3-pm.	
GOUVES	19/5/17.		Unit moved to ARRAS. left 11-30am. arrived 3-pm. A. and B bearer sub-divisions under Capt. R.H.Leigh and Capt.M.W.Paterson. respectively took over bearer posts from 2/1 London Field Amb. at 51.B. N.11.a.7.7. and MARLIERES and are attached to 48th Field Ambulance at TILLOY. Two large Motor Ambulance cars also attached to 48th Field Ambulance. Rest of unit parked in Hopital St.JEAN. in reserve. Severalshells apparently from a high velocity gun fell near building.	
ARRAS.	20/5/17.		Nothing to report.	
	21/5/17.		Town again shelled at night.	
	24/5/17		Lieut W. Q. McConnell Jones from No 37 C.C.S.	
	27/5/17		B Sect Bearer returned under Capt Paterson.	
	28/5/17		A sect Bearers Capt Leigh	
	30/5/17		Unit moved to DUISANS. Left 10.45 am arrived 1 pm	

J B Mawlo
Lt Col RAMC
Comm'g 2/1 FA

CONFIDENTIAL.

War Diary

of

Officer Commanding 50th Field Ambulance.

from 1st June 1917 to 30th June 1917.

(Volume 23.)

Vol 21
140/2230

COMMITTEE FOR THE
MEDICAL HISTORY OF THE WAR
Date -7 AUG. 1917

Army Form C. 2118.

WAR DIARY
INTELLIGENCE SUMMARY.
(Erase heading not required.)

Instructions regarding War Diaries and Intelligence Summaries are contained in F. S. Regs., Part II. and the Staff Manual respectively. Title pages will be prepared in manuscript.

Place	Date	Hour	Summary of Events and Information	Remarks and references to Appendices
THIGANE	1/6/17.		Lieut. W.H. Connell - R.A.M.C. takes over temporary Medical charge of 9th. Bn. North Staffords Regt. Lieut. Col. R.A.M.C. Commanding 50th. Field Ambulance.	
			Capt. S. CHILD - R.A.M.C. rejoins from temporary duty with 48th. F.A. (A.D.S.)	
"	3/6/17.		Unit moved to LICHTERVELT - Left 6 a.m. Arrived 10-30 a.m.	
LICHTERVELT	5/6/17.		2 O.R. proceed to Third Army Rest Camp for 14 days.	
			1 O.R. rejoins from VI C.R.S.	
"	6/6/17.		Capt. W.H. PATERSON - R.A.M.C. (S.R.) awarded Military Cross.	
			1 O.R. rejoins from temporary duty with 29th. Dvl. Gas School.	
"	7/6/17.		Unit moved to BELVAL - Left 5-15 a.m. Arrived 10-30 a.m.	
BELVAL	8/6/17.		Unit moved to COYECQUE - Left 8-30 a.m. Arrived 11-30 a.m.	
COYECQUE	9/6/17.		3 O.R. proceed on leave.	
"	12/6/17.		Lieut. J.S. LYMAN - M.R.C. - U.S. Army - joins unit for duty.	
"	13/6/17.		9 O.R. Reinforcements joined.	
"	14/6/17.		1 O.R. (A.S.C. M.T.) rejoined.	
"	15/6/17.		Lieut. W.M. McConnell - R.A.M.C. - Rejoined from temporary duty with 9th. North Staffords.	
			Lieut. J.C. LYMAN - M.R.C. - U.S. Army - takes over temporary Medical Charge of 10th. I.N. Lancs.	
			A.D.M.S. visited.	
"	17/6/17.		Capt. H.N. PATERSON. (M.C.) R.A.M.C. and 3 O.R. proceed on leave.	
"	19/6/17.		1 O.R. evacuated (sick) 2 O.R. proceed to First Army Rest Camp.	

Army Form C. 2118

WAR DIARY
or
INTELLIGENCE SUMMARY

(Erase heading not required.)

Instructions regarding War Diaries and Intelligence Summaries are contained in F. S. Regs, Part II. and the Staff Manual respectively. Title Pages will be prepared in manuscript.

Place	Date	Hour	Summary of Events and Information	Remarks and references to Appendices
Coyecque.	20/6/17.		A.D.M.S. visited. 5. O.R. reinforcements joined.	
	21/6/17.		Lieut.W.G.McConnell. R.A.M.C. takes over temporary medical charge of 10th L.N.Lancs. vice.Lieut. J.C.Lyman. M.R.C. U.S.Army.	
	22/6/17.		21 O.R. reinforcements joined.	
	23/6/17.		Unit moves to WITTES. Left 3-15 am. arrived 8-30am.	
Wittes.	24/6/17.		Unit moved to HONDEGHEM. Left 4-am. arrived 9-30am.	
Hondeghem.	25/6/17.		Unit moved to LOCRE. Left 7-30am arrived 2-pm. Lieut.C.F.Hardie. R.A.M.C. (T.C.) joined for duty.	
Locre.	27/6/17.		No.41278.Pte.R.Spence. R.A.M.C. reports to O.C. Reinforcements ROUEN. (Authy.D.A.G.Base.A.H. 2616. d/26/6/17.	
	28/6/17.		Unit moved to DRANOUTRE. Left 1-30pm. arrived 2-15pm. Main Dressing Station at Dranoutre.(M.35.c.3.2.) Advanced Dressing Stations at PARRAIN FARM (N.28.b.8.9.) and YONGE STREET (N.29.a.2.6.) Collecting Post at LINDENHOEK (N.27.c.8.8.) also Relay Posts at LUMM FARM (O.26.d.2.7.) ENFER WOOD. (O.31.b.6.9.) and STANSER CABARET (O.20.c.3.8.) taken over from 108th Field Ambulance. 36th (Ulster) Division.	
Dranoutre.	30/6/17.		A.D.M.S. visited.	
			Undermentioned N.C.O. and men awarded "Military Medal."	
			No.41869.Sergt.B.E.Radford. R.A.M.C.	
			" 38154.A/Lcpl.J.Huggett. "	
			" 38553. Pte. G. Crossley. "	
			" 81710. " H. Burt. "	

JBSneath Lieut.Col.R.A.M.C.
Commanding 50th Field Ambulance.

Vol 22

CONFIDENTIAL.

War Diary

of

Officer Commanding 50ᵗʰ Field Ambulance.

from 1ˢᵗ July 1917. to 31ˢᵗ July 1917.

(Volume 24.)

Medical

COMMITTEE FOR THE
MEDICAL HISTORY OF THE WAR
Date 10 SEP. 1917

Army Form C. 2118.

WAR DIARY
INTELLIGENCE SUMMARY.
(Erase heading not required.)

July 1917   (1)

Place	Date	Hour	Summary of Events and Information	Remarks and references to Appendices
DRANOUTRE	1/7/17.		War Diary of Lieut.Col.T.B.NICHOLLS.R.A.M.C.Commanding 50th.Field Ambulance,B.E.F.	
	1/7/17.		4 O.R.proceed on leave.	
	2/7/17.		Lieut.C.F.HARDIE posted to 48th.Field Ambulance for duty,and struck off the strength accordingly.	
	3/7/17.		Capt.M.W.PATERSON.M.C.returns from leave.	
	4/7/17.		Lieut.W.G.McCONNELL posted to temporary charge of 10th Battn.York & Lancs.Regt. H.M.The KING inspected the A.D.S. at PARRAIN FARM.	
	7/7/17.		3 O.R. proceeded on leave.No.39920 A/Cpl.HITCHINER.A.promoted A/Sergt.from 13/5/17. Bearer's of this unit relieved by 49th.F.Amb.in the Line Lieut.J.C.LYMAN.M.O.R.C. U.S.A. relieved Capt.R.H.LIEGH at A.D.S. C.O. proceeded on leave to U.K. Lieut.W.G.McCONNELL posted to permanent charge of 10th.York & Lancs.Regt.and struck off the strength accordingly	
	9/7/17.		Capt.H.B.G.RUSSELL joined and taken on the strength.He was immediately detailed for duty at IXth.Corps Headquarters;but remains on the strength of the Unit.	
	14/7/17.		3 O.R proceed on leave.	
	16/7/17.		A.D.S. at PARRAIN FARM handed over to 49th,Field Ambulance,this Unit retaining that at YONGE ST. 2 O.R. proceed to Second Army Rest Camp.	
	18/7/17.		C.O. returns from leave	
	19/7/17.		One man,A.S.C. H.T. evacuated sick.	
	20/7/17.		One Man R.A.M.C.evacuated sick.	
	21/7/17.		3 O.R. proceed on leave.One man detailed for temporary duty at D.H.Q.	
	22/7/17.		10 Casualties admitted from new type of Gas shell,containing,as far as I am able to ascertain,	

Army Form C. 2118.

WAR DIARY
or
INTELLIGENCE SUMMARY.

50th. F.A. July 1917.

(2)

(Erase heading not required.)

Instructions regarding War Diaries and Intelligence Summaries are contained in F.S. Regs., Part II. and the Staff Manual respectively. Title pages will be prepared in manuscript.

Place	Date	Hour	Summary of Events and Information	Remarks and references to Appendices
DRANOUTRE.	22/7/17 Cont.		Di-Chlor Ethyl Sulphide. The salient features were severe Conjunstivitis and blistering of the skin, particularly on the buttocks, penis and scrotum. The Box Respirator gave efficient protection. It has been suggested thatvthe blistering and conjunctivitis are caused by conveying the toxin on the hands. This was invsstigated. A number of men were put through Gas Drill and it was noticed that a considerable number of them rubbed their eyes on removing the masks.	
	23/7/17.		41 admissions from new shell gas, no fatal cases.	
	24/7/17.		34 Admissions from new gas, none fatal.	
	25/7/17.		11 Admissions from new gas, none fatal.	
	28/7/17.		One N.C.O. evacuated Scarlet Fever, contacts segregated.	
	29/7/17.		Medical Arrangements for attack by 63rd.Infy.Brigade issued by A.D.M.S. O.C.50th F.A. was detailed as being responsible for clearing the Line. Walking Wounded are to be dealt with under Corps arrangements. The following dispositions were made by me:- Two bearer subdivisions of this unit with one from 49th.F.A. under the command of Capt R.H.LIEGH were detailed to carry from the Line to WXXX WYTSCHAETE, Capt Liegh'S H.Q. to be at LUMM FARM. The Casualties to be carried from thence to the A.D.S's at YONGE STREET (50 F.A.) and PARRAIN FARM (49 F.A.) by Motor Ambulance Car, the cars to unload at each A.D.S. alternately and after the necessary attention to be cleared to the Main Dressing Station at DRANOUTRE (50 F.A.). Four Cars were placed at my disposal frpm 48th.F.A. The M.D.S. to be cleared by No.5 M.A.C. The services ot Captain R.V.POYSER, M.O.37th.Divisional Train, and Lieut.T.J.TAUNTON, M.O.37th. Divisional Ammunition Column were placed at my disposal after they had done their own duties. Officers were detailed as under. Bearers Capt.R.H.LIEGH. A.D.S. Capt.M.W.PATERSON.M.C. Lieut.J.C.LYMAN.M.O.R.O.,U.S.A.	

Army Form C. 2118.

(3)

WAR DIARY
or
INTELLIGENCE SUMMARY.

50 F.A. July 1917.

(Erase heading not required.)

Instructions regarding War Diaries and Intelligence Summaries are contained in F.S. Regs., Part II. and the Staff Manual respectively. Title pages will be prepared in manuscript.

Place	Date	Hour	Summary of Events and Information	Remarks and references to Appendices

DRANOUTRE.	29/7/17.		Main Dressing Station Capt.C.J.B.WAY.M.C.
			                                 Capt.R.W.POYSER.
			
			                                 Capt.S.CHILD.
			                                 Lieut.T.J.TAUNTON.
			
			 These officers to work as teams in relief of each other, with Lieut.E.M.Brown to attend to the slighter cases and the sick.	

	30/7/17.		Capt.R.H.LEECH proceeded up the line with his Bearer Subdivisions and Capt.Poyser and Lieut TAUNTON reported to me for instructions. I went up and inspected the arrangements, which appeared to be satisfactory. 4 O.R. proceeded to Second Army Rest Camp. Each Regimental aid post equipped with 5 Thomas' splints and Suspension Bars, 15 extra stretchers. A reserve of 50 stretchers and 50 blankets was divided equally between YONGE STREET A.D.S. and the bearer post at LUMM FARM.	
	31/7/17.		Attack at 3.50.a.m. very few casualties arrived at M.D.S. by 9.a.m. I went up to A.D.S. and found they were just beginning to come in. Owing to previous rain the road between LAMP POST CORNER (O 19 c.4.7. Sheet 28 S.W?) and WYTSCHAETE was impassable for large Ambulance Cars and could only be negotiated by Ford Ambulance Two Fords worked between LAMP POST CORNER and PECKHAM (N 30.a.3.7.-) where the cases were transferred to large cars for the rets of the journey to the A.D.S. A Light Railway ran past LAMP POST CORNER and the A.D.S. and a large number of stretcher cases were sent down in the returning trains. The wounded spoke very highly of this means of transport, and said that it was much more comfortable than a motor ambulance on a bad road. I went up as far as WYTCHAETE on three occasions this day and found the arrangements working without any hitch. The casualties were comparatively light only 102 stretcher cases being dealt with up to 9.p.m. The Main Dressing Station was visited during the day by the D.D.G.	

                                             Lieut Colonel, R.A.M.C.
                                      Commanding 50th. Field Ambulance, 37th. Division

Medical

CONFIDENTIAL. 140/364 Vol 23

War Diary

of

Officer Commanding, 50th Field Ambulance.

From 1st August 1917 To 31st August 1917.

(Volume 25.)

COMMITTEE FOR THE
MEDICAL HISTORY OF THE WAR
Date -1 OCT. 1917

Army Form C. 2118

WAR DIARY
or
INTELLIGENCE SUMMARY

(Erase heading not required.)

50th F.A. August 1917.

Instructions regarding War Diaries and Intelligence Summaries are contained in F.S. Regs., Part II. and the Staff Manual respectively. Title Pages will be prepared in manuscript.

Place	Date	Hour	Summary of Events and Information	Remarks and references to Appendices
Dranoutre	1/8/17.		War Diary of O.C. 50th Field Ambulance for the month of August 1917.	
			Capt M.W. Paterson M.C. detailed for temporary duty as D.A.D.M.S. Capt C.J.B. Way M.C. and Lieut E.M. Brown relieve Capt M.W. Paterson & Lieut J.C. Lymen M.O.R.C. U.S.A. at the Advanced Dressing Station.	
	2/8/17.		One O.R. returned from temporary duty at D.H.Q.	
	4/8/17.		Four other ranks proceed on leave. Capt F.E. Johnson} attached for temporary duty One N.C.O. (A.S.C.) joined for duty. Lieut A. Boothroyd} from 14th Division.	
	5/8/17.		One man R.A.M.C. evacuated (sick) One N.C.O. (H.T.) rejoined unit for duty. Advance party under Capt F.E. Johnson and Lieut E.M. Brown proceed to take over premises at Rue Benoit Cortoil BAILLEUL from 42nd Field Ambulance.	
	6/8/17.		Horses rendered surplus owing to new establishment returned to remounts.	
	7/8/17.		Remainder of Field Ambulance, less two Bearer Sub-divisions proceed to BAILLEUL to join advance party. Bearers and A.D.S. party relieved by advance party of 12th Australian Field Ambulance. Lieut E.M. Brown proceeded to take over charge of 37th D.A.C. and is struck off the strength accordingly.	
	8/8/17.		Lieut E.F.R.Alford M.C. joined the unit from 8th Bn. Somerset L.I. Handing over of Main Dressing Station at DRANOUTRE completed at 10.a.m. this morning. Bearers and the remainder of Field Ambulance proceed to BAILLEUL. Capt M.W. Paterson M.C. Capt S. Child and "B" Section detailed to proceed to HAGEDOORNE Camp Sheet 28. S.3.C.8.3. to prepare a hospital for isolating cases of suspected dysentery and contacts.	
Bailleul	9/8/17.		A.D.M.S. 37th Division inspected.	
	11/8/17.		Lieut J.C. Lyman M.O.R.C. U.S.A. proceeded to take over temporary medical charge of 13th Bn. The Rifle Brigade. Five O.R. proceed on leave. Five reinforcements joined.	
	12/8/17.		One N.C.O. (A.S.C.) H.T. returned to 37th Divisional Train for duty being surplus to establishment. No. 76973 Pte Fletcher J.H. appointed Lance Corporal with pay.	
	15/8/17.		One O.R. R.A.M.C. evacuated (sick)	
	16/8/17.		One O.R. R.A.M.C. evacuated (sick)	

WAR DIARY
or
INTELLIGENCE SUMMARY

(Erase heading not required.)

Army Form C. 2118

50th F.A. August 1917.

Place	Date	Hour	Summary of Events and Information	Remarks and references to Appendices
Bailleul.	17/8/17.		One O.R. R.A.M.C. evacuated (Sick)	
	18/8/17.		Capt F.E. Johnson and Lieut A. Boothroyd returned for duty to A.D.M.S. 14th Division. Fifteen O.R. proceed on leave under special allotment having been eighteen months or more without leave.	
	20/8/17.		No. 40250 Sergeant H.W. Walker transferred to R.F.C. on probation. Owing to the great frequency with which the Motor Ambulance Cars have been stopped by combat ranks requiring a "lift" it has been necessary to provide the drivers of these cars with written orders forbidding them to carry any but Sick and Wounded. This was reported to the A.D.M.S.	
	21/8/17.		No. 35926 Corporal Spicer W.S. promoted Lance Sergeant with pay.	
	22/8/17.		Cards and forms filled up by each Medical Officer giving particulars of commissions, qualifications and employments.	
	23/8/17.		A.D.M.S. inspected.	
			Capt C.J.B. Way M.C. proceeds on thirty days special leave to U.K.	
	25/8/17.		Four O.R. proceed on leave.	
			Capt M.W. Paterson M.C. proceeds to D.M.S. Second Army for duty and is struck off the strength accordingly.	
	26/8/17.		"C" Section sent to reinforce HAGEDOORNE Camp owing to the large amount of work to be done there.	
	27/8/17.		Four O.R. proceed to Second Army Rest Camp.	
	28/8/17.		D.D.M.S. 1X Corps inspected.	
	29/8/17.		A.D.M.S. 37th Division inspected.	
	31/8/17.		Nothing further to report since last entry.	
31/8/1917, In the Field.				

Lt Col R.A.M.C.
Commanding 50th Field Ambulance.

Army Form C. 2118.

WAR DIARY
INTELLIGENCE SUMMARY.
(Erase heading not required.)

Place	Date	Hour	Summary of Events and Information	Remarks and references to Appendices
In the Field.	31/8/17.		"R E M A R K S" A large amount of construction work has had to be done in this building. Two latrines with fly proof seats and concrete floors, ablution room with concrete floor, incinerator, drying room and spray bath have been made. The bath is being constructed with the incinerator as the source of heat for the water, this was first tried by this unit at DRANOUTRE and was found to be most successful, the present instalation works even better. A short description and sketch is appended. JBMelville. Lieut Col R.A.M.C, Commanding 50th Field Ambulance.	

CONFIDENTIAL.

Vol 24

War Diary

of

Officer Commanding, 50th Field Ambulance.

From 1st September 1917 To 30th September 1917.

(Volume 26.)

COMMITTEE FOR THE
MEDICAL HISTORY OF THE WAR
Date -5 NOV.1917

Army Form C. 2118.

WAR DIARY
~~or~~
INTELLIGENCE SUMMARY.
(Erase heading not required.)

Instructions regarding War Diaries and Intelligence Summaries are contained in F. S. Regs., Part II. and the Staff Manual respectively. Title pages will be prepared in manuscript.

Place	Date	Hour	Summary of Events and Information	Remarks and references to Appendices
Bailleul			War Diary of O.C. 50th Field Ambulance for the month of September 1917.	
	2/9/1917.		One O.R. R.A.M.C. joined for duty.	JBNeville Lt Col RAMC
	4/9/1917.		Six O.R. proceeded on leave to U.K.	
	6/9/1917.		Nine P.B. men joined for duty, to replace A.S.C. (H.T.) (Batmen) Eight A.S.C. (H.T.) men despatched to H.T.& S. Base Depot Havre under authority A.G.No.C/408/3 dated 23/8/1917.	
	7/9/1917.		No. 35926 L.Sergt Spicer W. R.A.M.C. promoted A/Sergt with pay 19/8/17 inclusive Authority D.G.M.S. No. B/1450/1387 dated 7/9/1917.	
	8/9/1917.		Lieut G.L. Watkins U.S. M.R.Corps joined for duty.	
	11/9/1917.		Five O.R. proceeded on leave to U.K.	
	12/9/1917.		One H.T.(A.S.C.) man despatched to H.T. & S. Base Depot Havre under authority A.G.No.C/408/3 dated 23/8/1917.	
	13/9/1917.		Two O.R. A.S.C.(H.T.) evacuated (Sick) Lieut J.C. Lyman U.S. M.R.Corps rejoined from temporary duty with 13th Bn. Rifle Brigade.	
	14/9/1917.		One P.B. man evacuated to base (Sick) Two large Motor Ambulance Cars report to 57th Field Ambulance for temporary duty.	
	15/9/1917.		Lieut J.C. Lyman U.S. M.R.Corps takes over permanent Medical Charge of 10th Bn. L.N.lancs.	
	17/9/1917.		One O.R. R.A.M.C. evacuated (Sick).	
	18/9/1917.		One O.R. (A.S.C.) H.T. joined for duty.	
	19/8/1917.		Eight O.R. proceeded on leave to U.K.	
	20/9/1917.		One large Motor Ambulance Car rejoins from temporary duty with 57th Field Ambulance. Lieut G.L. Watkins U.S. M.R.Corps proceeded to No. 2 C.C.S. for temporary duty.	
	22/9/1917.		Two Ford Ambulance Cars report to O.C. 49th Field Ambulance for duty.	
	24/9/1917.		Lieut G.L. Watkins U.S. M.R.Corps rejoined from temporary duty with No. 2 C.C.S. Capt H.E. Creswell M.C. R.A.M.C. joined for duty.	
	25/9/1917.		One O.R. R.A.M.C. evacuated (Sick).	
	26/9/1917.		Four O.R. proceeded on leave to U.K.	
	27/9/1917.		Capt C.J.B. Way M.C. R.A.M.C. returned from one months leave to U.K. Capt H.E. Creswell M.C. R.A.M.C. proceeded for temporary duty with 13th Bn. K.R.R.C.	
	28/9/1917.		Two large Motor Ambulance Cars report to O.C. 49th Field Ambulance for temporary duty.	
	30/9/1917.		Nothing further to report since last entry.	
30/9/1917. In the Field.				

JBNeville Lieut Col R.A.M.C.
Commanding 50th Field Ambulance.

2. BEARER SUB-DIVISIONS.

No rations were available from 112th Infantry Brgde sources for the bearers, after the rations carried were consumed, they had therefore to eat their emergency rations on the last day.

Thomas' splint proved useful. More might be issued to R.M.O's. The blanket carried by each bearer proved most useful and probably saved many men from dying of exposure. This measure might be adopted by the Regimental Stretcher Bearers with advantage.

The emergency carrying parties provided by the fighting troops were very awkward at handling wounded and carrying stretchers.

J.D.Nicolls.
Lt Col R.A.M.C.,
Commanding 50th Field Ambulance.

DRYING
+
BATH
ROOM

DRYING
+
BATH
ROOM

Diagrammatic Sketch of Drying & Bath Room

Heat furnished by Brick Incinerator & Thermo Syphon

Fig I

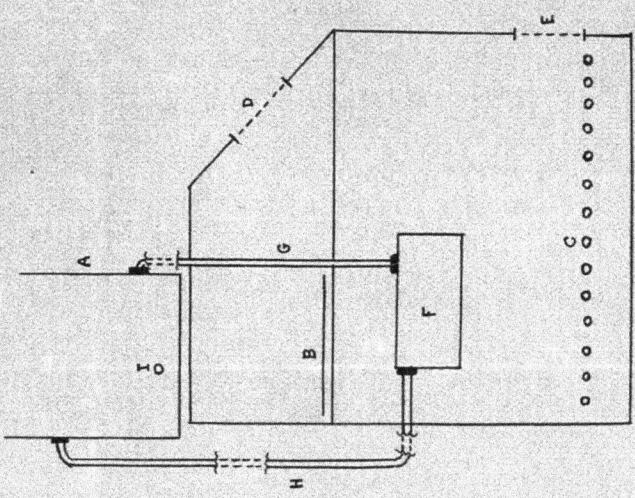

A = 100 gallon Tank
B = Tray for drying faecal matter before burning
C = Fire bars
D = Opening for feeding refuse
E = Opening for raking
F = Oil Drum boiler
G.H. = Thermo Syphon pipes
I = Tap

Vol 25

CONFIDENTIAL.

War Diary

of

Officer Commanding, 50th Field Ambulance

from 1st October 1917 to 31st October 1917.

(Volume 24)

COMMITTEE FOR THE
MEDICAL HISTORY OF THE WAR
Date -8 DEC. 1917

Army Form C. 2118

WAR DIARY
INTELLIGENCE SUMMARY
(Erase heading not required.)

Instructions regarding War Diaries and Intelligence Summaries are contained in F.S. Regs., Part II. and the Staff Manual respectively. Title Pages will be prepared in manuscript.

Place	Date	Hour	Summary of Events and Information	Remarks and references to Appendices
Bailleul			Diary of Lieut Col T.B. Nicholls R.A.M.C. Commanding 50th Field Ambulance B.E.F.	
"	1/10/17.		Lieut E.F.R. Alford M.C. R.A.M.C. proceeded on 14 days leave to U.K.	
"	2/10/17.		Four O.R. proceeded on leave to U.K.	
"	3/10/17.		Lieut T.F. Collins R.A.M.C. joined 50th F.A. for duty. 50 Bearers under No. 39921 Sergt G.W. Higgs R.A.M.C. report to O.C. 49th Field Ambulance for temporary duty.	
"	4/10/17.		No. 78228 Pte W.E. Lowe R.A.M.C. and No. 73258 Pte J. Moore R.A.M.C. Killed in Action. Two O.R. evacuated (Wounded) One O.R. evacuated (Sick)	
"	5/10/17.		No. 11574 Pte A.C.H. Symms R.A.M.C. Killed in Action. One O.R. evacuated (Wounded). One O.R. evacuated (Sick) 16 Bearers under No. 38169 Corpl Hollingworth R.A.M.C. report to O.C. 49th Field Ambulance for temporary duty.	
"	6/10/17.		One O.R. evacuated (Sick) One O.R. evacuated (Wounded) One O.R. joined 50th Field Ambulance for duty.	
"	8/10/17.		One O.R. evacuated (Sick) Capt H.E. Creswell M.C. R.A.M.C. rejoins from temporary duty with 13th Bn. K.R.R.Corps.	
"	9/10/17.		No. 23485 Pte J.Smith R.A.M.C. Killed in Action. Four O.R. evacuated (Wounded) Three O.R. proceeded on leave to U.K.	
"	11/10/17.		Capt H.E. Creswell M.C. R.A.M.C. reports to O.C. 49th Field Ambulance for temporary duty.	
"	12/10/17.		Capt S. Child R.A.M.C. (T.F.) left unit for temporary duty as O.C. No. 81 Sanitary Section. 30 Bearers and Corporal T.Weston under No. 35596 Sergt W.S. Spicer R.A.M.C. report to O.C. 49th Field Ambulance for temporary duty. Hospital shelled. All patients cleared and sheltered at No. 2 C.C.S. for the night.	

Army Form C. 2118

WAR DIARY
INTELLIGENCE SUMMARY
(Erase heading not required.)

Place	Date	Hour	Summary of Events and Information	Remarks and references to Appendices
Bailleul.	13/10/17.		Two O.R. evacuated (Sick) One R.A.M.C. and one A.S.C.(H.T.). One O.R. (M.T.) A.S.C. and Ford Motor Ambulance Car No. 20 evacuated to base.	
"	14/10/17.		Capt H.E. Creswell M.C. R.A.M.C. takes over permanent Medical Charge of 10th Bn. Royal Fusiliers	
"	16/10/17.		All Bearers temporarily attached to 49th Field Ambulance rejoin unit. Capt C.J.B. Way M.C. R.A.M.C. reports to A.D.M.S., 37th Division for temporary duty. Three O.R. proceeded on leave to U.K. One O.R. (A.S.C.) H.T. and One O.R. (A.S.C.) M.T. joined 50th Field Ambulance for duty.	
"	17/10/17.		Lieut E.F.R. Alford M.C. R.A.M.C. rejoined from leave.	
"	18/10/17.		10 O.R. R.A.M.C. joined 50th Field Ambulance for duty.	
"	22/10/17.		Commanding Officer's Parade held.	
"	23/10/17.		Lieut T.F. Collins R.A.M.C. left unit, having been "Dismissed from His Majesty's Service" by F.G.C.M. held on 13/10/17. Three O.R. proceeded on leave to U.K.	
"	24/10/17.		Commanding Officer's Parade held.	
"	25/10/17.		Lieut E.F.R. Alford M.C. R.A.M.C. reports to O.C. No. 44 C.C.S. for temporary duty.	
"	26/10/17.		Hospital shelled. All patients cleared. Capt R.H. Leigh R.A.M.C. proceeded on One months leave to U.K. A.D.M.S., 37th Division visited unit.	
"	27/10/17.		Capt C.J.B. Way M.C. R.A.M.C. rejoined unit from temporary duty with A.D.M.S., 37th Division.	
"	30/10/17.		Hospital shelled. All patients cleared. Three O.R. proceeded on leave to U.K. Lieut W.K. Black U.S. M.R.C. joined 50th Field Ambulance for duty.	
"	31/10/17.		Commanding Officer's Parade held. A.D.M.S., 37th Division visited.	

Lt Col R.A.M.C.
Commanding 50th Field Ambulance.

CONFIDENTIAL.

140/678

Vol 26

War Diary

of

Officer Commanding, 50th Field Ambulance

from 1st November 1917 to 30th November 1917.

(Volume 28)

COMMITTEE FOR THE
MEDICAL HISTORY OF THE WAR
Date 17 JAN. 1918

Army Form C. 2118

WAR DIARY
or
INTELLIGENCE SUMMARY

(Erase heading not required.)

Instructions regarding War Diaries and Intelligence Summaries are contained in F.S. Regs., Part II. and the Staff Manual respectively. Title Pages will be prepared in manuscript.

Place	Date	Hour	Summary of Events and Information	Remarks and references to Appendices
			War Diary of O.C. 50th. Field Ambulance for month of November 1917.	
BAILLEUL	1/11/17.		Lt.Col. Nicholls, R.A.M.C., (O.C. 50th. Fd. Amb.) admitted to Fd. Amb. sick. Commdg: 50th. Fd. Amb. Capt. R.A.M.C.	
do	2/11/18		Capt. C.J.B.WAY, M.C., R.A.M.C. assumes temporary command of unit. Unit inspected, on parade, by A.D.M.S. 37th. Division. No. 33354, Pte. A.E.Smith, R.A.M.C. and No. 77644, Pte. W.S.Jenkins, R.A.M.C. awarded Military Medal. Capt. E.F.R.ALFORD, M.C., R.A.M.C., rejoined from temporary duty with 44th. C.C.S. HAEGEDOORNE Dysentery Camp retaken over by 50th. Fd. Amb. from 133rd. Fd. Amb.	
do	5/11/17		Capt. W.B.WISHART, R.A.M.C. 48th. Fd. Amb. reports for temporary duty.	
do	6/11/17		Sergt. B.E.RADFORD, R.A.M.C. appointed A/S.Sgt. (Authy: D.G.M.S. no. 1450/1607 d/5.11.17. Lt.Col. Nicholls, R.A.M.C. (O.C. 50th. Fd. Amb.) discharged from hospital and proceeded on one month's Special Leave to the U.K. 3 O.R. proceed on leave.	
do	7/11/17		Capt. W.B.WISHART, R.A.M.C., rejoined 48th. Fd. Amb. for duty. Capt. J.A.QUIN, R.A.M.C., joined for duty.	
do	9/11/17		3 N.C.O.s and 60 bearers report to O.C. 48th. Fd. Amb. for temporary duty. 9 R.A.M.C. Reinforcements joined.	
do	13/11/17.		4 O.R. proceed on leave.	
do	14/11/17.		1 O.R. ("P.B." attached) evacuated to C.C.S. sick.	
do	15/11/17.		1 O.R. (R.A.M.C.) and 1 O.R.(A.S.C.) evacuated to C.C.S. (sick)	
do	16/11/17.		Divisional Commander inspected the hospital.	
do	17/11/17.		Unit moved from BAILLEUL and took over premises occupied by Tent-Sub-Division of 48th. Field Ambulance at MAGILLIGAN CAMP (S.9.d.) and KEERSEBROM (S.10.d) where a Main Dressing Station and Divisional Rest Station were formed.	
MAGILLIGAN CAMP.	20/11/17.		3 O.R. proceed on leave.	
do	23/11/17.		Capt. H.B.G.RUSSELL, R.A.M.C., appntd.D.A.D.M.S. IX Corps and struck off strength.	

Army Form C. 2118

WAR DIARY
or
INTELLIGENCE SUMMARY
(Erase heading not required.)

Instructions regarding War Diaries and Intelligence Summaries are contained in F. S. Regs., Part II. and the Staff Manual respectively. Title Pages will be prepared in manuscript.

Place	Date	Hour	Summary of Events and Information	Remarks and references to Appendices
MAGILLIGAN CAMP.	24/11/17.		1 O.R. (R.A.M.C.) evacuated to C.C.S. sick.	
do	25/11/17.		1 O.R. (A.S.C.) joined for duty.	
do	27/11/17.		Capt. R.H.LEIGH, R.A.M.C., returned from leave.	
			Lt. & Qr. M.W.COLAHAN, R.A.M.C. and 3 O.R. proceed on leave.	
do	29/11/17.		Lieut. G.L.WATKINS, M.O.R.C., U.S.A. reported to O.C. 48th. Fd. Amb. for temporary duty.	
do	30/11/17.		Capt. S.CHILD, R.A.M.C., rejoined from temporary duty as O.C. 81st. Sanitary Section.	
			Capt. J.A.QUIN, R.A.M.C., took over temporary Medical Charge of 13th. Bn. Royal Fusiliers.	

30/11/1917.
In the Field.

[signature]
Captain R.A.M.C.
Commanding 50th. Field Ambulance.

CONFIDENTIAL

War Diary

of

Officer Commanding, 50th Field Ambulance

From 1st December 1914 to 31st December 1914.

(Volume 29)

WAR DIARY
INTELLIGENCE SUMMARY

(Erase heading not required.)

Army Form C. 2118

War Diary of O.C. 50th. Field Ambulance for month of December 1917.

JB Meeuls
Lt.Col. R.A.M.C.
Commanding 50th. Field Ambulance.

Place	Date	Hour	Summary of Events and Information	Remarks and references to Appendices
MAGILLIGAN Camp.	3/12/17.		3 O.R. proceeded on leave	
do	4/12/17.		1 O.R. evacuated (wounded)	
			15 O.R. under Captain S. CHILD, R.A.M.C. (T.F.) took over IX Corps Officers' Rest Station from 59th. Field Ambulance, 19th. Division.	
			Lieut. G.L. WATKINS, M.O.R.C., U.S.A. rejoined from temporary duty with 48th. Field Ambulance.	
do	5/12/17.		15 O.R. R.A.M.C. joined for temporary duty from 49th. Field Ambulance.	
do	7/12/17.		1 O.R. proceeded on leave. Medical Board held for purpose of reclassifying P.B. men in area.	
			20 O.R. R.A.M.C. transferred for duty with No. 9 H.A.GROUP.	
			1 O.R. R.A.M.C. reported to D.D.M.S. IX Corps for temporary duty.	
do	8/12/17.		1 O.R. evacuated (sick)	
			C.O. returned from leave.	
do	10/12/17.		2 O.R. proceed on leave.	
do	11/12/17.		1 O.R. evacuated (sick)	
do	13/12/17.		1 O.R. evacuated (sick)	
			Captain R.A. AUSTIN, R.A.M.C. (S.R.) posted to No. 50 Field Amb; doing duty with D.D.M.S. IX Corps.	
do	14/12/17.		1 O.R. evacuated (sick)	
do	15/12/17.		1 O.R. evacuated (sick)	
			Captain J.A. QUIN, R.A.M.C. evacuated to Base (sick)	
do	16/12/17.		3 P.B. men attached transferred to respective Base Depots having been reclassified "A" by Medical Board held on 7/12/17.	
do	17/12/17.		Lieut. G.L. WATKINS, M.O.R.C., U.S.A. takes over temporary Medical charge of 8th. Bn. Lincoln Regt.	
do	19/12/17.		3 O.R. proceed on leave.	
do	23/12/17.		Captain W.A. MILNER, R.A.M.C. (T.F.) joined for duty.	
			1 O.R. proceeds on leave.	

WAR DIARY
or
INTELLIGENCE-SUMMARY

(Erase heading not required.)

Army Form C. 2118

Place	Date	Hour	Summary of Events and Information	Remarks and references to Appendices
MAGILLIGAN Camp.	23/12/17.		4 hospitals under command of O.C. 50th. Field Ambulance inspected by G.O.C 57th. Division.	
do	24/12/17.		2 O.R. proceed on leave.	
do	27/12/17.		1 O.R. rejoined from temporary duty with D.D.M.S. IX Corps. Nothing further to report.	
	31/12/17.		In the Field.	

E.D.Nicholls
Lieut.Col. R.A.M.C.
Commanding 50th. Field Ambulance.

"CONFIDENTIAL."

War Diary

of

Officer Commanding, 50th Field Ambulance

From 1st January 1918 to 31st January 1918.

(Volume 30)

COMMITTEE FOR THE
MEDICAL HISTORY OF THE WAR
Date -4 MAR. 1918

WAR DIARY

~~INTELLIGENCE SUMMARY~~

(Erase heading not required.)

Army Form C. 2118

Instructions regarding War Diaries and Intelligence Summaries are contained in F.S. Regs., Part II. and the Staff Manual respectively. Title Pages will be prepared in manuscript.

War Diary of O.C. 50th. Field Ambulance for month of January, 1918.

Place	Date	Hour	Summary of Events and Information	Remarks and references to Appendices
MAGILLIGAN CAMP.	1/1/18.		No. 76973 L/Cpl. J.H.Fletcher, R.A.M.C. appointed A/Corporal (with pay) from 9/12/17.	
			O.Neville Lt. Col. R.A.M.C. Commanding 50th. Field Ambulance.	
do	1/1/18.		Lt. & Q.M. Colahan, R.A.M.C. Mentioned in Dispatches.(authority, supplement to London Gazette dated 1/1/18.)	
do	3/1/18.		Capt. R.H.Leigh, R.A.M.C. Awarded Military Cross.(Authority New Year's Honours Gazette d/1/1/18)	
do			2 men category "B" joined for duty.	
do			Capt. C.J.B.Way (M.C.) took charge of HAEGEDOORNE (Dysentery) Camp.	
do	4/1/18.		1 O.R. evacuated (sick).	
do	7/1/18.		1 O.R. Proceeded on leave.	
do			5 O.R. Proceeded on leave.	
do			No. 38885, Sgt.Mjr. G.A.Medlock, R.A.M.C. awarded Meritorious Service Medal. (Authority, New Year's Honours Gazette dated 1/1/18)	
do	9/1/18.		1 O.R. evacuated (sick).	
do	10/1/18.		N.C.O's and men of 49th. Fd. Amb. attached for temporary duty returned to their unit.	
do	10/1/18.		3 O.R. proceeded on leave.	
do	11/1/18.		Unit moved and took over premises at No. 8 Rue de College, BAILLEUL, from 60th. Fd. Amb. Main Dressing Station at MAGILLIGAN Camp and Divisional Rest Station at KEERSEBROM handed over to 4th. Australian Fd. Amb. (4th Australian Division).	
BAILLEUL	13/1/18.		12 O.R. proceeded on leave.	
do	18/1/18.		1 O.R. evacuated (sick).	
do			Capt. T.B.Watson R.A.M.C. (T.C.) and Capt. W.Craig, R.A.M.C. (T.C.) joined for duty.	
do	19/1/18.		Capt. W.A.Milner (T.F.) posted to permanent Medical charge of 4th Middlesex Regt.	
do	20/1/18.		9 O.R. proceeded on leave.	
do	22/1/18.		Capt. R.H.Leigh M.C. - R.A.M.C., reported to A.D.M.S. 37th Division for temporary duty.	
do	23/1/18.		2 O.R. proceeded on leave.	
do	25/1/18.		1 O.R. evacuated (sick)	

WAR DIARY or INTELLIGENCE SUMMARY

Army Form C. 2118

Place	Date	Hour	Summary of Events and Information	Remarks and references to Appendices
BAILLEUL	27/1/18		7 O.R. proceeded on leave.	
do	31/1/18		Nothing further to report.	

Lt. Col. R.A.M.C.
Commanding 50th Field Ambulance.

LIST OF HONOURS AND REWARDS UP TO 31st. JANUARY, 1918.

Capt. H.N.Stafford.	R.A.M.C.	Military Cross. (awarded)
" C.J.B.Way.	R.A.M.C.	DO.
" M.W.Paterson.	R.A.M.C.	DO.
" R.H.Leigh.	R.A.M.C.	DO.
No.38885. Sgt.Mjr. G.A.Medlock.	R.A.M.C.	Meritorious Service Medal.
No.35593. Sgt. W.T.Williams.	R.A.M.C.	DO.
No.35593. " W.T.Williams.	R.A.M.C.	Military Medal. (awarded)
No.37749. " G. Gordon.	R.A.M.C.	DO.
No.41869. " B.E.Radford.	R.A.M.C.	DO.
No.36039. Cpl. J.B.Richardson.	R.A.M.C.	DO.
No.38154. " J.Huggett.	R.A.M.C.	DO.
No.38155. Pte. T.Hatton.	R.A.M.C.	DO.
No.39489. " R.A.Ives.	R.A.M.C.	DO.
No.44108. " T.J.Molloy.	R.A.M.C.	DO.
No.38553. " G.W.Crossley.	R.A.M.C.	DO.
No.83710. " H.Burt.	R.A.M.C.	DO.
No.38166. " W.B.Halley.	R.A.M.C.	DO.
No.35589. " H.H.Smalley.	R.A.M.C.	DO.
No.37483. " H.C.M.Hooper.	R.A.M.C.	DO.
No.33354. " A.E.Smith.	R.A.M.C.	DO.
No.77644. " W.S.Jenkins.	R.A.M.C.	DO.
No.M2/055079. Dr. A.S.Wellman.	A.S.C.(M.T.)	DO.

Lt. Col. R.A.M.C.
Commanding 50th Field Ambulance.

CONFIDENTIAL.

War Diary

of

Officer Commanding, 50th Field Ambulance

From 1st February 1918.
To 28th February 1918.

(Volume 31)

Army Form C. 2118

WAR DIARY
or
INTELLIGENCE SUMMARY
(Erase heading not required.)

Instructions regarding War Diaries and Intelligence Summaries are contained in F. S. Regs., Part II. and the Staff Manual respectively. Title Pages will be prepared in manuscript.

Place	Date	Hour	Summary of Events and Information	Remarks and references to Appendices
			War Diary of O.C. 50th. Field Ambulance for month of February 1918.	
BAILLEUL	1/2/18.		1 O.R. (R.A.M.C.) rejoined unit for duty from base. JMeakle Lt.Col. R.A.M.C. Commanding 50th. Field Ambulance.	
do	3/2/18.		4 O.R. proceed on leave.	
			Captain E.F.R.ALFORD, M.C., R.A.M.C. transferred to No. 44 C.C.S. for duty.	
			2 "B" Personnel joined for duty.	
do	7/2/18.		Captain R.H.LEIGH, M.C., R.A.M.C. rejoined unit from temporary duty with A.D.M.S. 37th. Division.	
			10 R.A.M.C. Reinforcements joined for duty.	
do	8/2/18.		Captain S.CHILD, R.A.M.C. transferred as O.C. No.5 Motor Ambulance Convoy.	
			1 O.R. (R.A.M.C.) evacuated sick.	
do	10/2/18.		5 O.R. proceed on leave.	
do	12/2/18.		Advanced Party of 30 O.R. under Captain R.H.LEIGH, M.C., R.A.M.C. proceeded to take over Advanced Dressing Station and Forward Posts occupied by 62nd. Field Ambulance.	
			Lieut. J.T.HILL, R.A.M.C. joined for duty.	

Army Form C. 2118

WAR DIARY
or
INTELLIGENCE-SUMMARY
(Erase heading not required.)

Instructions regarding War Diaries and Intelligence Summaries are contained in F.S. Regs., Part II. and the Staff Manual respectively. Title Pages will be prepared in manuscript.

Place	Date	Hour	Summary of Events and Information	Remarks and references to Appendices
BAILLEUL	13/2/18.		Unit moved moved from BAILLEUL and took over Main Dressing Station at WOODCOTE HOUSE (I.20.c.4.2.) - Advanced Dressing Station (I.30.a.5.0) and all Forward Posts occupied by 62nd. Field Ambulance, also Sick Collecting Station, LA CLYTTE.	
WOODCOTE HOUSE.	16/2/18.		Lieut. W.SCOTT, M.O.R.C., U.S.A. joined unit for temporary duty from 48th. Field Ambulance.	
do	17/2/18.		6 O.R. proceed on leave.	
do	19/2/18.		Lieut.G.L.WATKINS, M.O.R.C., U.S.A. rejoined unit from temporary duty with 8th. Lincolns.	
do	21/2/18.		1 O.R. evacuated (sick).	
			Stretcher Bearers in front area relieved.	
			Captain W.CRAIG, R.A.M.C. relieved Captain R.H.LEIGH, M.C., R.A.M.C. as Officer i/c Advanced Dressing Station and Bearers.	
do	24/2/18.		Lieut.G.L.WATKINS, M.O.R.C., U.S.A. and 6 O.R. proceed on leave.	
			Lieut. W.SCOTT, M.O.R.C., U.S.A. rejoined 48th. Field Ambulance for duty.	
			4 R.A.M.C. Reinforcements joined for duty. (2 B I, 2 B II)	
do	25/2/18.		Captain C.J.B.WAY, M.C., R.A.M.C. and party rejoined unit from temporary duty at XXII Corps School for Medical Officers.	
			1 O.R. (A.S.C. H.T.) evacuated sick.	
do	26/2/18.		16 O.R. slightly gassed (mustard gas)	
do	28/2/18.		Nothing further to report.	

JBNeville
Lt.Col. R.A.M.C.
Commanding 50th. Field Ambulance.

CONFIDENTIAL.

Vol 30

War Diary

of

Officer Commanding, 50th Field Ambulance

From 1st March 1918 to 31st March 1918

(Volume 32.)

COMMITTEE FOR THE
MEDICAL HISTORY OF THE WAR
Date 12 MAY 1918

Army Form C. 2118.

WAR DIARY
or
INTELLIGENCE SUMMARY.
(Erase heading not required.)

Instructions regarding War Diaries and Intelligence Summaries are contained in F. S. Regs., Part II. and the Staff Manual respectively. Title pages will be prepared in manuscript.

Place	Date	Hour	Summary of Events and Information	Remarks and references to Appendices
WOODCOTE HOUSE.	1/3/18		War Diary of No. 50th Field Ambulance for month of March 1918. Capt. C.J.B. Way. M.C. - R.A.M.C. relieved Capt. W. Craig - R.A.M.C. as Officer i/c Advanced Dressing Station, Reavers. OBNeville Lt.Col. Rawe Commanding 50th Field Ambulance	
"	5/3/18		Reavers in Front Area relieved. OBZ	
"	6/3/18		10 O.R. proceeded on leave. OBZ	
"	6/3/18		1 O.R. (A.S.C. H.T.) joined for duty. OBZ	
"	7/3/18		"PRECAUTIONARY ACTION" received. 1 Reaver Sub-division, 2 Motor Ambulance Cars & 2 Hand Ambulances reported from No. 3rd Amb. for temporary duty.	
"	8/3/18		1 O.R. rejoined from temporary duty with No.11 C.C.S. OBZ Capt. R.H. LEIGH. M.C. - R.A.M.C. relieved Capt. C.J.B. WAY. M.C. - R.A.M.C. as Officer i/c Advanced Dressing Station and Reavers. Reavers in Front Area relieved. 20 additional Reavers reported for temporary duty from 48th 3rd Amb. OBZ 1 O.R. (R.A.M.C.) evacuated (wounded) 1 O.R. (A.S.C. H.T.) evacuated (sick)	

A.D.&.S./Forms/F.118.

Army Form C. 2118.

WAR DIARY
or
INTELLIGENCE SUMMARY.
(Erase heading not required.)

Instructions regarding War Diaries and Intelligence Summaries are contained in F. S. Regs., Part II. and the Staff Manual respectively. Title pages will be prepared in manuscript.

Place	Date	Hour	Summary of Events and Information	Remarks and references to Appendices
WOODCOTE HOUSE	9/3/18		Lieut. M.B. QUNN - R.A.M.C., temporarily attached, proceeded to Advanced Dressing Station for duty.	
	11/3/18		6 reinforcements (R.A.M.C.) joined for duty. JBG	
			1 O.R. proceeded on leave.	
			Gas Alarm received 8-59 p.m.	
			Gas Alarm OFF received 9-88 p.m. (Drift from Shelsea (wing Westerly wind) JBG	
			1 O.T.P. evacuated (sick) JBG	
	12/3/18		Lt. G.L. WATKINS, M.O.R.C., U.S.A. returned from leave. JBG	
	14/3/18		1 O.R. (A.S.C. H.T.) joined for duty. JBG	
	15/3/18		Capt. C.J.B. WAY - M.C. - R.A.M.C. relieved Capt. R.H. LEIGH - M.C. - R.A.M.C. as Officer i/c Advanced Dressing Station & Reserve.	
			Lieut J.T. HILL - R.A.M.C. proceeded to Advanced Dressing Station for duty.	
			Reserve in Front Area relieved.	
	16/3/18		Lieut M.B. QUNN - R.A.M.C. returned from duty at Advanced Dressing Station JBG	
			1 O.R. proceeded on leave. JBG	

Army Form C. 2118.

WAR DIARY
or
INTELLIGENCE SUMMARY.

(Erase heading not required.)

Instructions regarding War Diaries and Intelligence Summaries are contained in F. S. Regs., Part II. and the Staff Manual respectively. Title pages will be prepared in manuscript.

Place	Date	Hour	Summary of Events and Information	Remarks and references to Appendices
WOODCOTE HOUSE	19/3/18		1 O.R. (R.A.M.C) evacuated (wounded). JBG	
	20/3/18		1 O.R. ('B' personnel) evacuated (sick) JBG	
	22/3/18		Lieut. G.L. WATKINS - M.O.R.C - U.S.A. relieved Major C.J.B. WAY - M.C. - R.A.M.C. as Officer i/c Advanced Dressing Station & Divisional Reserve in Front Area relieved. JBG	
			N° 2-1-4-49 Pte. W.J. JACKSON - R.A.M.C. ⎫	
			" 38161 " A.F. HARRIS - do - ⎬ Awarded "Military Medal" JBG	
			" 344415 " H.S. LILLEY - do - ⎪ (Authority:- XXII Corps A.4164/4 dy/8.3.18	
			" 38115 " A. COAD - do - ⎭	
	24/3/18		1 O.R. ('B' personnel) evacuated (sick) JBG	
	25/3/18		Captain M.J. CASSERLY - R.A.M.C. (T.C.) joined for duty. JBG	
			Lieut. G.L. WATKINS - M.O.R.C - U.S.A. transferred to medical charge of 2nd Batt. Tanks Bgde.	
			Captain W. CRAIG - R.A.M.C relieved Lieut. G.L. WATKINS - M.O.R.C - U.S.A. as Officer i/c Advanced Dressing Station & Reserve. JBG	
			Capt. W. CRAIG - R.A.M.C took over temporary charge of Advanced Dressing Station & Reserve. JBG	
	26/3/18		Capt. M.J. CASSERLY - R.A.M.C. relieved Capt. W. CRAIG - R.A.M.C. as Officer i/c XXII Corps Officers Rest Station, EPERLECQUES Advanced Dressing Station & Reserve. JBG	

Army Form C. 2118.

WAR DIARY
or
INTELLIGENCE SUMMARY.
(Erase heading not required.)

Instructions regarding War Diaries and Intelligence Summaries are contained in F. S. Regs., Part II. and the Staff Manual respectively. Title pages will be prepared in manuscript.

Place	Date	Hour	Summary of Events and Information	Remarks and references to Appendices
WOODCOTE HOUSE	28/3/18		Main Dressing Station at WOODCOTE HOUSE (I. 20. a. 2. d.), Advanced Dressing Station (I. 30. a. 5. d) and all found posts in occupation by personnel of this unit handed over to 1/1 West Riding Field Ambulance (49th Division). Sick Collecting Station, LA CLYTTE, handed over to Area Commandant. Unit moved to WARATAH CAMP (G. H. central) Capt. W. CRAIG. R.A.M.C. appointed unit from temporary duty as Officer i/c XXII Corps Officers' Rest Station, EPERLECQUES. Lieut. J. T. HILL. R.A.M.C. rejoined unit from temporary duty as M.O. i/c 10th Royal Fusiliers O.B.Z.	
WARATAH CAMP	29/3/18		Unit entrained at HOPOUTRE Siding, Near POPERINGHE. Train departed 3·55 p.m.	
	30/3/18		Arrived MONDICOURT Station 9 a.m. Unit marched from MONDICOURT to billets in old Huts standing on MARIEUX - SARTON Road – arrived 12·30 p.m.	
MARIEUX	31/3/18		Unit moved from billets in MARIEUX - SARTON Road to HUMBERCAMPS. Left 2·30 p.m. arrived 6 p.m.	

J.O.Newcastle/Lt.
F.Col. Paul.
Commanding 50 Field Ambulance

2353 Wt. W2544/1454 700,000 5/15 D. D. & L. A.D.S.S./Forms/C. 2118.

SECRET.   50th. FIELD AMBULANCE.

Reference Map.   MEDICAL ARRANGEMENTS.
Sheet 28
1/40,000.

Wounded are carried from Left & Right R.A.P.s, at J.20.b.6.4. and
J.20.d.3.7. respectively, to Bearer Post at BODMIN COPSE
(J.19.b.8.1.) via DUMBARTON TRACKS - thence to the Advanced
Dressing Station at CANADA STREET (I.30.a.5.0) via DUMBARTON
TRACKS, and then by wheeled stretchers to the CABSTAND (I.28.b.8.6
via MORLAND AVENUE. An alternative route to the CABSTAND is via
PERTH AVENUE, which does not touch the Advanced Dressing Station.
At the CABSTAND cases are loaded on Motor Ambulance Cars, which
convey the patients to the Main Dressing Station at WOODCOTE
HOUSE(I.20.c.4.2.)

A Walking Wounded Collecting Station has been established at the
CABSTAND (I.28.b.8.6). The route for Walking Wounded from the
R.A.P.s to the CABSTAND is as under:-

DUMBARTON LAKES - PERTH AVENUE - STIRLING TRACK -
PLUMERS DRIVE SOUTH - CABSTAND.

Numbers of R.A.M.C. personnel occupying the different posts are
as under:-

Right R.A.P.   ------   4 men.
Left R.A.P.   -------   8 men.
BODMIN COPSE   ------   1 N.C.O. 16 men.
ADVANCED DRESSING STATION ----- 1 Officer, 2 N.C.O., 18 men.
CABSTAND   -------- 1 N.C.O., 4 men.

Bearer Posts are also located at OBSERVATORY RIDGE
(I.24.c.9.3.) and TANK VIEW (I.24.d.7.6). These are used
chiefly for casualties in Artillery etc. personnel.
Numbers of R.A.M.C. personnel in occupation are as under:-

OBSERVATORY RIDGE   -----   4 men.
TANK VIEW   -----------   4 men.

%/%/%/%/%/%/%/%/%/%/%/%/%/%/%/%/%/%

                                    Lieut.Col. R.A.M.C.
1st. March 1918.   Commanding 50th. Field Ambulance.

CONFIDENTIAL.

War Diary

of

Officer Commanding, 50th Field Ambulance.

From 1st April 1918 to 30th April 1918.

(Volume 33)

Army Form C. 2118.

Instructions regarding War Diaries and Intelligence Summaries are contained in F. S. Regs., Part II. and the Staff Manual respectively. Title pages will be prepared in manuscript.

WAR DIARY
INTELLIGENCE SUMMARY.
(Erase heading not required.)

Place	Date	Hour	Summary of Events and Information	Remarks and references to Appendices
			War Diary of O.C. 50th Field Ambulance for month of April 1918.	
HUMBERCAMP	1/4/18		2/3rd West Riding Field Ambulance (62nd Division) relieved in the line.	
			O.B. New Ms., Lt. Col. Paine Commanding 50th Field Ambulance	
			Advanced Dressing Station at FONQUEVILLERS – E.M. & S.O. duties up and all Forward Posts occupied by 2/3rd West Riding F. Amb. taken over under Major T.H. LEIGH – M.C. R.A.M.C. in charge.	
			All heaves of not going must relieved.	
			Capts. M.J. CASSERLEY - R.A.M.C. and Lieut. J.T. HILL - R.A.M.C. proceeded to Forward Area for duty.	
COUIN	2/4/18		Unit moved to COUIN (J.1.C.0.0) left 8 p.m. arrived 9-30 p.m. ODS	
			Control Station for both Horse ration Transport established at BIENVILLERS under instructions of A.D.M.S. 37th Division.	
			Dressing Roads for walking wounded erected from line to GOMMECOURT through FONQUEVILLERS to New Dressing Station at SOUASTRE. ODS	
	3/4/18		Reserve Division of 4th Australian Field Ambulance (4th Div.) reported for temporary duty.	
			1 Bearer Sub-Division of 49th Field Ambulance reported for temporary duty.	
				JBL

WAR DIARY

INTELLIGENCE SUMMARY.

Army Form C. 2118.

Place	Date	Hour	Summary of Events and Information	Remarks and references to Appendices
COUIN	4/4/18		O.C. attended conference at office of A.D.M.S, 37th Division.	
	5/4/18		2 extra M.A. Cars detailed to proceed to FONQUEVILLERS for duty. 1 O.R. (R.A.M.C) evacuated wounded. 6 Horse Ambulances (3 of this unit and 3 of 4th Amb. 3rd Amb. attd) detailed for duty in forward area to convey walking wounded to main Dressing Station, SOUASTRE. Major C.J.B.WAY - M.C. - R.A.M.C. relieved Major T.H.LEIGH - M.C. - R.A.M.C. as officer i/c A.D.S. & Bearers.	
	6/4/18		Capt. W. CRAIG - R.A.M.C and Captain T.B. WATSON - R.A.M.C. proceeded to Forward Area for duty. Captain M.J. CASSERLEY - R.A.M.C. returned to H.Q. Personnel at Advanced Dressing Station relieved.	
	8/4/18		Lieut J.T. HILL - R.A.M.C. took over temporary medical charge of 13th & 20th Rifle Brigade. No 36634 Sgt. T.C. EVANS - R.A.M.C. and No 93812 Corpl. W.J. HUNT - R.A.M.C. detailed to supervise preventive treatment of French troops at 111th and 63rd Advanced Brigade H.Q. respectively.	
	10/4/18		Two Bearer Squads of 46th 3rd Amb. relieved by two squads of this unit at Rifle T.A.P. Left Brigade (K.6.d.3.f.) new line of evacuation being Rifle Aid Post - Relay Post K.6.b.3.t - along Tramway - Relay Post K.5.a.6.6 - GOMMECOURT - FONQUEVILLERS.	
	11/4/18		Major R.H. LEIGH - M.C. - R.A.M.C. relieved Major C.J.B. WAY - M.C. - R.A.M.C. as officer i/c A.D.S. & Bearers.	

Army Form C. 2118.

WAR DIARY
INTELLIGENCE SUMMARY.
(Erase heading not required.)

Place	Date	Hour	Summary of Events and Information	Remarks and references to Appendices
COUIN	11/4/16		Capt. M.J. CASSERLEY - R.A.M.C. proceeded to A.D.S. for duty. Capt. W. CRAIG - R.A.M.C. and Capt. T.B. WATSON - R.A.M.C. attached to 2nd Aust. H.Q. 1 O.R. (R.A.M.C.) evacuated (wounded). JRC	
	12/4/16		Lt. M.B. GUNN - R.A.M.C. proceeded to Advanced Dressing Station for duty. C.O. attended Conference at Office of A.D.M.S. 34th Division. JRC	
	13/4/16		Arrangements completed for evacuation of wounded from Right Centre Brigade and Australian Brigade to Advanced Dressing Station at SAILLY-AU-BOIS (48th Field Amb.) Route of evacuation, of which Lieut. M.B. GUNN - R.A.M.C. is in charge, is as follows:- Regt. Aid Posts at K.9.b.5.1 (Cheese pd) and K.9.b.6.1 - by hand carriage to Relay Post at K.9.c.3.4. - by hand carriage to Relay Post at K.10.b.4.4. - thence to Advanced Dressing Station at SAILLY-AU-BOIS (J.16.a.9.4.) There arrangements made to conform with those of Divisional Front. 1 Rear Sub-Division of 48th Field Ambulance returned for temporary duty.	
	14/4/16		1 Rear Sub-Division of this unit reported to O.C. 48th Field Ambulance for temporary duty in Right Centre and Right Brigade Sectors of line. JRC 1 Rear Sub-Division of 48th Field Ambulance, temporarily attached, returned to unit. 1 Rear Sub-Division of 49th Field Ambulance reported for temporary duty. JRC	
	15/4/16		1 Rear Sub-Division of this unit, temporarily attached to 48th Field Ambulance for duty, returned. 2 Rear Sub-Divisions of 49th Field Ambulance, temporarily attached to this Field Amb., returned to unit. JRC	

Army Form C. 2118.

WAR DIARY
INTELLIGENCE SUMMARY.
(Erase heading not required.)

Instructions regarding War Diaries and Intelligence Summaries are contained in F.S. Regs., Part II. and the Staff Manual respectively. Title pages will be prepared in manuscript.

Place	Date	Hour	Summary of Events and Information	Remarks and references to Appendices
COUIN	16/4/18		This unit relieved in the line by 1/5th East Lancs Field Ambulance (4th of Divisions) Advanced Dressing Station at FONQUEVILLERS - E.M.D.O. Sheet 57D and all forward posts relieved by this unit handed over. All bearers of this unit relieved by bearers of 1/5th East Lancs Field Ambulance. Relief completed by 6 a.m. All bearers and Advanced Dressing Station personnel reported to Amb. H.Q. at COUIN (J.1.C.0.0. Sheet 57D) on relief. Unit moved to MARIEUX - Left 7 p.m. arrived 4 p.m.	
MARIEUX	17/4/18		1 Bearer Sub-Division and 3 large Motor Ambulance Cars reported to U.S. 49th Field Ambulance for temporary duty.	
	25/4/18		Unit moved from MARIEUX to PAS - Left 8 a.m. arrived 10 a.m.	
"PAS - EN- ARTOIS"	27/4/18		Handed over Command to Major C/B W H M.C.	
			O B Newcastle Lt. Col. Commanding 50th Field Amb.	
	27/4/18		Major C. J. B. WAY - M.E. R.A.M.C. took over command of 50th Field Ambulance from Lieut. Col. T. B. NICHOLLS - R.A.M.C. who was transferred for duty as U.C. 53rd Field Ambulance. Murray Major R.A.M.C. Commanding 50th Fd Amb.	

/

Army Form C. 2118.

WAR DIARY
INTELLIGENCE SUMMARY

(Erase heading not required.)

Place	Date	Hour	Summary of Events and Information	Remarks and references to Appendices
PAS-EN ARTOIS	28/4/16		Captain M. J. CASSERLY - R.A.M.C. transferred to permanent medical charge of 124th Brigade - R.F.A.	
	30/4/16		Nothing further to report.	

O.N.Rway
Major R.A.M.C.
Commanding 50th Field Ambulance

CONFIDENTIAL.

W.D. 32
140/2293.

War Diary

of

Officer Commanding, 50th Field Ambulance.

From 1st May 1918.
To 31st May 1918.

(Volume 34.)

M

WAR DIARY

INTELLIGENCE SUMMARY

Army Form C. 2118.

Place	Date	Hour	Summary of Events and Information	Remarks and references to Appendices
PAS-EN-ARTOIS	1/5/18		War Diary of U.C. 50th Field Ambulance for month of May 1918.	
			C W Gray	
			Major R.A.M.C.	
			Commanding 50th Field Ambulance	
			1 O.R. (R.A.M.C.) evacuated (sick)	
	2/5/18		1 O.R. (R.A.M.C.) returned for duty. CWBW	
			1 O.R. (R.A.M.C.) evacuated (sick)	
			Captain W. CRAIG - R.A.M.C. evacuated (sick) CWBW	
	4/5/18		1 O.R. (R.A.M.C.) evacuated (sick) CWBW	
			No 39180 a/Cpl. J.M.WATT. R.A.M.C. appointed a/Sergeant with pay from 5/4/18. (Authority:-	
			D.Q.M.S./B/1450/365 dated 2.5.18) CWBW	
			No 44108 A/L/Cpl. F.J. MOLLOY - R.A.M.C. appointed a/Corporal with pay from 5/4/18 (Authority:-	
			D.Q.M.S./B/1450/365 dated 2.5.18) CWBW	
			No 39660. Pte. J.T.HYLAND - R.A.M.C. left unit to report to U.S. Personnel Supply Park,	
			Alconbury, Hunts. England, for duty. (Authy:- T.R.A.F. No 14590S (A) 2/5. 4.18 and A.G. 2150/41 (6)	
			N/5.9. 1.18 CWBW	
			Captain H.W. BAYLY - R.A.M.C. (T.F.) } Joined for duty. CWBW	
			Captain J. PRICHARD - R.A.M.C. (T.C.) }	
	5/5/18		1 O.R. (R.A.M.C.) evacuated (sick) CWBW	

Army Form C. 2118.

WAR DIARY
INTELLIGENCE SUMMARY.
(Erase heading not required.)

Instructions regarding War Diaries and Intelligence Summaries are contained in F. S. Regs., Part II. and the Staff Manual respectively. Title pages will be prepared in manuscript.

Place	Date	Hour	Summary of Events and Information	Remarks and references to Appendices
PAS-en-ARTOIS	6/5/18		Captain J. PRICHARD - R.A.M.C. (T.C.) transferred to permanent medical charge of 40th Labour Group. [WRW]	
	8/5/18		1/Lieut. T.W. COOK - M.O.R.C. - U.S.A. joined for duty. [WRW] 2.O.R. (R.A.M.C.) evacuated (sick)	
	9/5/18		Handed over command to Lieut. Col. G.D. HINDLEY - R.A.M.C. O.B.E. Lieut. Col. G.D. HINDLEY - R.A.M.C. took over command of 50th Field Ambulance from Major E.J.B. WAY, M.C., R.A.M.C. [signed] WRWay Major R.A.M.C. Commanding 50th Field Ambulance [signed] G.D. Hindley Lieut. Col. R.A.M.C. Commanding 50th Field Ambulance	G.D.H
	10/5/18		1 O.R. evacuated (sick)	
	13/5/18		1/Lieut. T.W. COOK, M.O.R.C. U.S.A. took over temporary medical charge of 9th Works Coy. N⁰ 34736 Pte. H.J. GRIFFITHS - R.A.M.C. appointed A/Corporal with pay from 10.5.18 (authority:- D.A.M.S/BJ/450/2411 of 10.5.18) 1 O.R. (R.A.M.C.) evacuated (sick)	G.D.H
			N⁰ 48193 Pte. R. MILBURN - R.A.M.C. appointed A/Lance Corporal with pay from 18.5.18	G.D.H

Army Form C. 2118.

WAR DIARY
or
INTELLIGENCE SUMMARY.
(Erase heading not required.)

Instructions regarding War Diaries and Intelligence Summaries are contained in F. S. Regs., Part II. and the Staff Manual respectively. Title pages will be prepared in manuscript.

Place	Date	Hour	Summary of Events and Information	Remarks and references to Appendices
PAS-EN-ARTOIS	14/5/18		1 O.R. (R.A.M.C.) evacuated (sick)	G.D.H.
	16/5/18		1 O.R. (R.A.M.C.) rejoined for duty.	G.D.H.
	17/5/18.		Unit moved from PAS-EN-ARTOIS to AUTHIE and took over IV Corps Rest Station at AUTHIE MILL from 2/3rd West Riding Field Ambulance (62nd Division) Capt E. E. MACKAY - R.A.M.C. joined for duty. Major C.J.B. WAY - M.C. - R.A.M.C. proceeded on 14 days Special Leave to the U.K.	G.D.H.
AUTHIE	18/5/18		1/Lieut T.W. COOK - M.O.R.C. - U.S.A. posted to permanent medical charge of 9th Mule Coy. 1 Reserve Sub-Division and 3 large Motor Ambulance Cars reported from temporary duty with 49th Field Ambulance.	G.D.H.
	21/5/18		1 O.R. (R.A.M.C.) evacuated (sick)	G.D.H.
	22/5/18		200 Respirators worn by all ranks for one hour	G.D.H.
	23/5/18		200 Respirators worn by all ranks for one hour Lecture delivered by Divl. Gas Officer to all ranks.	G.D.H.
	24/5/18		200 Respirators worn by all ranks for one hour. 6 R.A.M.C. Reinforcements joined for duty.	G.D.H.
	25/5/18		200 Respirators worn by all ranks for one hour. Medical Board assembled for reclassification of Category "B" men. President:- Major T.H. LEIGH M.C. - R.A.M.C. Member:- Capt. E.E. MACKAY - R.A.M.C.	G.D.H.

Army Form C. 2118.

WAR DIARY
INTELLIGENCE SUMMARY.
(Erase heading not required.)

Instructions regarding War Diaries and Intelligence Summaries are contained in F. S. Regs., Part II. and the Staff Manual respectively. Title pages will be prepared in manuscript.

Place	Date	Hour	Summary of Events and Information	Remarks and references to Appendices
AUTHIE	27/5/18		1 O.R. ("B" Personnel) evacuated (sick)	G.D.H.
	28/5/18		Gas Respirators worn by all ranks for one hour.	G.D.H.
			1 O.R. (A.S.C. M.T) joined for duty.	
	29/5/18		No. 10051, L/Cpl. W.C. WALKER - R.A.M.C. appointed a/Corporal with pay from 5.5.18 (Authority :- D.A.M.S./B/1450/506 d/6.5.18).	G.D.H.
	30/5/18		Captain W.S. PIPER - M.O.R.C. - U.S.A. joined for duty.	G.D.H.
	31/5/18		1 O.R. (R.A.M.C.) proceeded on Special Leave to U.K.	G.D.H.

G.D Hindley
Major R.A.M.C.
Commanding 50th Field Ambulance

CONFIDENTIAL.

Vol 33

War Diary

of

Officer Commanding, 50th Field Ambulance

From 1st June 1918 30th June 1918.

(Volume 55.)

WAR DIARY
INTELLIGENCE SUMMARY

Army Form C. 2118.

Place	Date	Hour	Summary of Events and Information	Remarks and references to Appendices
AUTHIE	2/6/18		War Diary of U.C. 50th Field Ambulance for month of June 1918. No 34646 Qr. H.A. SCOTT - R.A.M.C. appointed A/R.S.M. with pay from 2.6.18. C.D. Hindley Lieut. Col. R.A.M.C. Commanding 50th Field Ambulance	G.D.H.
	3/6/18		10 R.A.M.C. reinforcements joined for duty.	G.D.H.
	4/6/18		All Horse Transport and A.S.C. (M.T.) personnel, under Captain H.W. BAYLY - R.A.M.C., moved in advance by road. Left 9-30 p.m.	G.D.H.
	5/6/18		TV Corps Rest Station, AUTHIE Mill, handed over to 3rd New Zealand Field Ambulance.	G.D.H.
	6/6/18		Division being in G.H.Q. Reserve Unit moved from AUTHIE to ST. PIERRE-A-GOUY. Personnel by bus. Buses left 10-30 a.m. arrived 4 p.m. 1 O.R. R.A.M.C. evacuated (sick)	G.D.H.
ST. PIERRE-A-GOUY.	10/6/18		Unit moved from ST. PIERRE-A-GOUY to NEUVILLE-SOUS-LOSVILLY (CONTY AREA) Personnel by bus. Left 8 a.m arrived 5 p.m.	G.D.H.
NEUVILLE-SOUS-LOSVILLY	13/6/18		1 O.R. (R.A.M.C) evacuated (sick) 1 O.R. (A.S.C.M.T) evacuated (sick) Captain W.S. PIPER - M.O.R.C. U.S.A evacuated (sick) 1 O.R. (R.A.M.C.) evacuated (sick)	G.D.H.

Army Form C. 2118.

WAR DIARY
INTELLIGENCE SUMMARY.
(Erase heading not required.)

Instructions regarding War Diaries and Intelligence Summaries are contained in F. S. Regs., Part II. and the Staff Manual respectively. Title pages will be prepared in manuscript.

Place	Date	Hour	Summary of Events and Information	Remarks and references to Appendices
NEUVILLE - SOUS - LOEUILLY	16/6/18		1 O.R. (R.A.M.C) evacuated (sick).	G.D.H.
			Lieut. M.B. Gunn. R.A.M.C. left unit. Dismissed H. McSween by F.G.C.M. held 3/6/18.	
	19/6/18		1 O.R. (A.S.C.H.T) joined for duty.	G.D.H.
	23/6/18		Unit moved from NEUVILLE-SOUS-LOEUILLY to HENU (IV Corps Area). Ry. train to MONDICOURT, thence by road to HENU. Left 6 a.m. arrived 2 p.m.	G.D.H.
HENU	"		1 O.R. (R.A.M.C) evacuated (sick).	
	24/6/18		3 Bearer Sub-Divisions under Major C.J.B. Way. M.C. - R.A.M.C. left unit to relieve bearers of 2/2nd West Riding Field Ambulance (62nd Divn.) in the line.	G.D.H.
	27/6/18		1 O.R. (R.A.M.C) evacuated (sick).	
			H.Q. & West Riding Field Ambulance relieved in the line. Advanced Dressing Station at BIENVILLERS (E. & D. central) and all Forward Posts taken over.	G.D.H.
			Field Amb. H.Q. moved from HENU to Advanced Dressing Station, BIENVILLERS.	
BIENVILLERS	28/6/18		1 Bearer Sub-Division reported from 4/5th Field Ambulance for temporary duty.	
			1 Bearer Sub-Division reported from 49th Field Ambulance for temporary duty.	
			2 Large Motor Amb. Cars reported from 49th Field Ambulance for temporary duty.	G.D.H.
	29/6/18		Advanced Dressing Station moved from E. & D. central (sheet 57D) to E.8.a.9.8 (sheet 57D) BIENVILLERS.	G.D.H.
	30/6/18		Nothing further to report.	G.D.H.

G. D. Hindley Lieut. Col. R.A.M.C.
Commanding 50th Field Ambulance.

CONFIDENTIAL.

Vol 34
149/3/31.

War Diary

of

Officer Commanding, 50th Field Ambulance

From 1st July 1918 to 31st July 1918

(Volume 36.)

WAR DIARY

INTELLIGENCE SUMMARY.

Army Form C. 2118.

Place	Date	Hour	Summary of Events and Information	Remarks and references to Appendices
BIENVILLERS	1/7/18		War Diary of 146. 50th Field Ambulance for month of July 1918. All Reserves in Front Area relieved.	G.D.H.
			G.D. Hindley Lieut Col. RAMC Commanding 50th Field Ambulance.	
	2/7/18		1 O.R. (R.A.M.C.) evacuated sick	G.D.H.
	3/7/18		Capt W. Craig. R.A.M.C. rejoined for duty. 1 O.R. (R.A.M.C.) joined for duty.	G.D.H.
	4/7/18		1 O.R. (A.S.C. M.T.) evacuated sick. 1st Lt F.O. Stone - M.O.R.C. U.S.A. joined for duty. Capt H.W. Bayly - R.A.M.C. (T.F.) transferred to medical charge of 293rd Army Brigade R.F.A.	G.D.H.
	6/7/18		1 O.R. (R.A.M.C.) evacuated sick.	G.D.H.
			All Reserves in Front Area relieved.	
	9/7/18		1 O.R. (A.S.C. M.T.) evacuated sick	G.D.H.
	11/7/18		1 O.R. (A.S.C. M.T.) joined for duty	G.D.H.
	14/7/18		5 O.R. R.A.M.C. Reinforcements joined for duty.	G.D.H.
	16/7/18		All Reserves in Front Area relieved.	G.D.H.
			1 O.R. (R.A.M.C.) rejoined for duty.	

Army Form C. 2118.

WAR DIARY
or
INTELLIGENCE SUMMARY.
(Erase heading not required.)

Instructions regarding War Diaries and Intelligence Summaries are contained in F. S. Regs., Part II. and the Staff Manual respectively. Title pages will be prepared in manuscript.

Place	Date	Hour	Summary of Events and Information	Remarks and references to Appendices
BIENVILLERS	23/4/18		Minor operation carried out by 4th Middlesex Regt. on night 23rd/24th July. R.A.M.C. Bearer Posts reinforced and an Ambulance Car loaded on LA BAYELLE Road to convey cases to Car Loading Post, FONQUEVILLERS (E.M.L. X.1 Sheet 51c) Casualties were very slight.	G.D.H.
	24/4/18		All Reserve in Front Area relieved	G.D.H.
	25/4/18		No 43367, Pte. W. REED. R.A.M.C. transferred to office of D.E.M.S. for duty.	G.D.H.
	26/4/18		1 O.R. (A.S.C. H.T) joined for duty. Lieut. Col. G. D. HINDLEY. M.E. R.A.M.C. proceeded on leave to PARIS and handed over command of 50th Field Ambulance temporarily to Major C. J. B. WAY. M.E. R.A.M.C. G.D. Hindley Lt Col. O.C. 50th F.Amb.	
	28/4/18		Major C.J.B. WAY. M.E. R.A.M.C. took over temporary command of 50th Field Amb. from Lieut. Col. G. D. HINDLEY. M.E. R.A.M.C. C J B Way Major RAMC Commanding 50th Field Ambulance	
	29/4/18		2 R.A.M.C. Reinforcements joined for duty.	
	30/4/18		Lieut. B. E. COBB. M.O.R.C. - U.S.A. joined for duty.	

WAR DIARY
or
INTELLIGENCE SUMMARY
(Erase heading not required.)

Army Form C. 2118

Place	Date	Hour	Summary of Events and Information	Remarks and references to Appendices
BIENVILLERS	30/7/18		Minor operation carried out by 1st & 2nd Essex Regt. on night 30/31st July. R.A.M.C. Bearer Posts reinforced and two Ambulance Cars - one located on ESSARTS - HANNESCAMPS Road (E.18.c.5.2 sheet 57D) and one at CRUCIFIX CORNER (E.19.c.8.2 sheet 57D) to convey cases, via HANNESCAMPS, to A.D.S. BIENVILLERS (E.8.a.9.8 sheet 57D).	
	31/7/18		Nothing further to report.	

D.T.Spring
Major R.A.M.C.
Commanding 50th Field Ambulance

CONFIDENTIAL.

WR 35
140/3200.

War Diary

of

Officer Commanding, 50th Field Ambulance

From 1st August 1918 To 31st August 1918.

(Volume 37.)

Army Form C. 2118.

WAR DIARY
INTELLIGENCE SUMMARY.
(Erase heading not required.)

Instructions regarding War Diaries and Intelligence Summaries are contained in F. S. Regs., Part II. and the Staff Manual respectively. Title pages will be prepared in manuscript.

Place	Date	Hour	Summary of Events and Information	Remarks and references to Appendices
BIENVILLERS	1/8/18		War Diary of U.S. 50th Field Ambulance for month of August 1918. All Ranks in Front Area relieved. G.R.Snow Major R.A.M.C. a/c U.S. 50th Field Ambulance.	
	2/8/18		1 O.R. (A.S.C. H.T) evacuated, sick.	
	3/8/18		1 N.R. (A.S.C. H.T) joined for duty.	
	5/8/18		No. 16333 Staff Sgt. W. McKENNA - R.A.M.C. joined for duty from No. 6 Stationary Hospital. Lieut. Col. G. D. HINDLEY - M.C. - R.A.M.C returned from Paris leave and resumed command of 50th Field Ambulance from Major G.J.B. WAY - M.C. - R.A.M.C(A/C)	G.D.H.
	6/8/18		No. 36622 Staff Sgt. A. GILLESPIE - R.A.M.C. transferred to No. 6 Stationary Hospital for duty.	G.D.H.
	7/8/18		1 O.R. (R.A.M.C) rejoined for duty.	G.D.H.
	8/8/18		Major T.H. LEIGH - M.C. - R.A.M.C., Capts. & 2 M.W. COLAHAN - R.A.M.C and 3 O.R.s proceeded on leave.	Q.D.H.
			1 O.R. (R.A.M.C) evacuated, sick.	G.D.H
			1 O.R. (A.S.C. H.T) evacuated, sick.	G.D.H
	9/8/18		1 O.R. (R.A.M.C) evacuated, sick.	G.D.H
			All Ranks in Front Area relieved.	G.D.H.
	11/8/18		2 O.R. proceeded on leave to Paris.	G.D.H.

Army Form C. 2118.

WAR DIARY
INTELLIGENCE SUMMARY.
(Erase heading not required.)

Instructions regarding War Diaries and Intelligence Summaries are contained in F. S. Regs., Part II. and the Staff Manual respectively. Title pages will be prepared in manuscript.

Place	Date	Hour	Summary of Events and Information	Remarks and references to Appendices
BIENVILLERS	12/8/18		1 O.R. (A.S.C. M.T) went to Divⁿ Workshop and thence to Base with unserviceable M.T. Enl. Ambulance Car.	G.D.H.
	13/8/18		Lieut. F.O. STONE - M.O.R.C. - U.S.A. took over temporary medical charge of 4th Bⁿ Middlesex Regt.	G.D.H.
	14/8/18		Lieut. W.M. RICHARDS - R.A.M.C. joined for duty.	G.D.H.
			1 O.R. (R.A.M.C) evacuated sick.	
	16/8/18		6 O.R. proceeded on leave.	G.D.H.
	18/8/18		1 O.R. (A.S.C. H.T) joined for duty.	G.D.H.
			1 O.R. (A.S.C. H.T) rejoined for duty.	
	19/8/18		1 O.R. (R.A.M.C) joined for duty.	G.D.H.
			All Reserves in front Area relieved.	
	20/8/18		1 O.R. (R.A.M.C) evacuated sick.	G.D.H.
	21/8/18		1 O.R. (A.S.C. M.T) evacuated sick.	G.D.H.
			Division attacked at 4.55 a.m. Main Dressing Station was at SOUASTRE (49th Dⁿ Amb) and A.D.S. (this unit) was at FONQUEVILLERS. Rearw H.Q. & Car Loading Post at ESSARTS Crucifix. Rearw collecting Station from BUCQUOY - ABLAINZEVELLE Road. 34th Field Ambulance cleared by 9 a.m. - Field cleared by 5 p.m.	
	22/8/18		4 O.R. proceeded on leave.	G.D.H.

Army Form C. 2118.

WAR DIARY
or
INTELLIGENCE SUMMARY.
(Erase heading not required.)

Instructions regarding War Diaries and Intelligence Summaries are contained in F. S. Regs., Part II. and the Staff Manual respectively. Title pages will be prepared in manuscript.

Place	Date	Hour	Summary of Events and Information	Remarks and references to Appendices
BIENVILLERS	20/8/18	-	No. 26693, Pte G.H. Davies - R.A.M.C. transferred to 130th Field Amb. for duty	G.D.H.
	22/8/18		I.O.R. proceeded on 1 month's re-engagement leave.	G.D.H.
			I.O.R. (R.A.M.C.) evacuated sick.	
	23/8/18	3 a.m.	Bearer H.Q. & Car Loading Post moved to between LOGEAST WOOD and BUCQUOY Crucifix. Bearers collecting from ACHIET-LE-GRAND Line. ZERO hour 11 a.m. 37th Divl. Casualties cleared by 5 p.m. Field cleared by 3 a.m. 24th. A.D.S. moved from FONQUEVILLERS to ESSARTS Crucifix.	G.D.H.
			{Bearer A.D.S. at BIENVILLERS handed over to 46th Field Amb. for evac to Walking Wounded Main Dressing}	
	24/8/18	9 a.m.	Bearer H.Q. & Car Loading Post moved to old German Dug-out ½ mile W. of ACHIET-LE-GRAND. Bearers collecting from BIEFVILLERS-SAPIGNIES Line.	G.D.H.
		11 a.m.	Bearer H.Q. & Car Loading Post moved to X Roads between BIHUCOURT and ACHIET-LE-GRAND.	
	25/8/18	-	Bearers collecting from SAPIGNIES-FAVREUIL-BIEFVILLERS Sector. A.D.S. moved from ESSARTS Crucifix to Railway Station, ACHIET-LE-GRAND. Major T.H. LEIGH - M.C. - R.A.M.C. and Capt. + 2nd M.W. COLAHAN - R.A.M.C. returned from leave.	G.D.H.
			I.O.R. (R.A.M.C.) evacuated sick.	
	26/8/18	9 a.m.	No. 38261, Pte W.E. KNIGHT - R.A.M.C. } killed in action " 38157, " W. HARDY - do - } " 49578, " J. FIRTH - do - }	G.D.H.

Army Form C. 2118.

WAR DIARY
or
INTELLIGENCE SUMMARY.
(Erase heading not required.)

Instructions regarding War Diaries and Intelligence Summaries are contained in F. S. Regs., Part II. and the Staff Manual respectively. Title pages will be prepared in manuscript.

Place	Date	Hour	Summary of Events and Information	Remarks and references to Appendices
BIENVILLERS	27/8/16	3 a.m.	Divl. Front clear – Division relieved – Bearers returned to units and Bearer H.Q. to A.D.S. at ACHIET-LE-GRAND.	G.D.H.
		3 p.m.	Field Amb. H.Q. moved from BIENVILLERS to ACHIET-LE-GRAND. 6 O.R. (R.A.M.C) evacuated wounded (1 since died of wounds) 1 O.R. (A.S.C. M.T) evacuated wounded 1 O.R. (A.S.C. M.T) joined for duty with Ford Car to replace unserviceable one evacuated to Base.	G.D.H.
ACHIET-LE-GRAND	29/8/16		4 O.R. proceeded on leave. 1 O.R. (R.A.M.C.) rejoined for duty.	G.D.H.
	30/8/16		3 R.A.M.C. reinforcements joined for duty. 1 O.R. (A.S.C. M.T) joined for duty with Sunbeam Ambulance Car to replace one damaged by shell fire, evacuated to Base.	G.D.H.
	31/8/16		Major F.O. STONE – M.O.R.C. – U.S.A posted to permanent medical charge of 4th Bn Middlesex Regt.	G.D.H.

G.D. Hindley
Lieut Col RAMC
Commanding 50 Field Ambulance

Confidential

War Diary

of

Officer Commanding 50th Field Ambulance.

From 1st September 1918 to 30th September 1918.

Volume 36.

WAR DIARY
INTELLIGENCE SUMMARY.
(Erase heading not required.)

Army Form C. 2118.

Instructions regarding War Diaries and Intelligence Summaries are contained in F. S. Regs., Part II. and the Staff Manual respectively. Title pages will be prepared in manuscript.

Place	Date	Hour	Summary of Events and Information	Remarks and references to Appendices
ACHIET-LE-GRAND	1/9/18		War Diary of O.C. 50th Field Ambulance for month of September 1918.	G.D.H.
			Transport and Q.M. Stores moved from LOGEAST WOOD to the "WHITE HOUSE".	
			C.D. Hindley Lt. Col. R.A.M.C. O.C. 50th Field Ambulance.	
	3/9/18		Lt. B.E. COBB M.O.R.C. U.S.A. evacuated (sick)	G.D.H.
			Field Ambulance H.Qrs. moved from FONCET-LE-GRAND to BEUGNATRE.	
			13th Field Ambulance (57 Div) retired in dawn and all forward posts on night 3/4 September. On completion of relief, O.C. 50 F.A. became responsible for evacuation of line from R.A.Ps to Main Dressing Station.	
			Advanced Dressing Station opened at LEBUCQUIERE (I.30.a.6.6 about 57a.)	
	4/9/18		Field Ambulance H.Qrs. moved from BEUGNATRE to LEBUCQUIERE.	G.D.H.
			H.O.R. proceeded on leave.	
			2 Bearer Sub-divisions and 2 Large M.A. Cars reported for temporary duty from both 48th and 149th Field Ambulances.	

Army Form C. 2118.

WAR DIARY
INTELLIGENCE SUMMARY
(Erase heading not required.)

Place	Date	Hour	Summary of Events and Information	Remarks and references to Appendices
LEBUCQUIERE	9/9/18		1.O.R. (A.S.C. M.T) transferred to 39 Div. Ayres. Transport Coy.	G.D.H.
	10/9/18		Field Ambulance Hd Qrs moves from LEBUCQUIERE to BERTINCOURT (Pl. c.5.9 Sheet 57.a) Advanced dressing station Remains at RUYAULCOURT (P10. a. 5.5. sheet 57 c)	G.D.H.
BERTINCOURT	11/9/18		H.O.R. (R.A.M.C.) Proceeded on leave	G.D.H.
	12/9/18		1. O.R. (R.A.M.C) join for duty	G.D.H.
	12/9/18		1. O.R. (A.S.C. M.T) Joined for duty	G.D.H.
	13/9/18		1. O.R (A.S.C M.T) Joined for duty	G.D.H.
	15/9/18		Field Ambulance Hd Qrs moves from BERTINCOURT (Pl. c F.9 sheet 57 c) to RUYAULCOURT (P10.a 5.5 sheet 50.c)	G.D.H.
RUYAULCOURT	18/9/18		H. O. R. Proceeded on leave	G.D.H.
	15/9/18		1. N.C.O. (R.A.M.C) joined for duty	
		9pm	Our lorries Gas schedules at Clayton Cross (Q.S.a. 1.9 sheet 57 c) Bearer Hd Qrs in dug out near (Q.S.a. 2.3. Sheet 57c)	
			1.O.R (R.A.M.C) evacuated (sick).	G.D.H.

WAR DIARY
INTELLIGENCE SUMMARY

Army Form C. 2118.

(Erase heading not required.)

Instructions regarding War Diaries and Intelligence Summaries are contained in F. S. Regs., Part II. and the Staff Manual respectively. Title pages will be prepared in manuscript.

Place	Date	Hour	Summary of Events and Information	Remarks and references to Appendices
RUYAULCOURT	19/9/18		1. O.R. (R.A.M.C.) evacuated (wounded)	G.D.H.
	20/9/18		6532 Pte W.B. Leask R.F.A att'd A.S.C (M.T.) transferred to A.V.C. for duty with O.C. No 2 Veterinary Hospital	G.D.H.
	21/9/18		Unit moved from RUYAULCOURT to LE BARQUE M/12 a 3.9. 2 Bearer Sub. Divisions (Hq' F.A.) & M.A. Cars rejoined Unit	G.D.H.
LE BARQUE	22/9/18		1. O.R. (R.A.M.C.) evacuated (sick)	G.D.H.
	23/9/18		T/259152 Pte H.A. BARBER A.S.C (M.T.) transferred to A.S.C. Base Depot (as unfit for service at the Front). 16323 S/Sergt (A.R.M.S) W. McKENNA R.A.M.C. transferred for duty as Q.M.Sgt with 1/3 East Lancs. Fd. Amber. O.C. O.R. Granted on Leave 1. O.R. " " " to PARIS. 2 Bearer Sub. Divisions (H8 F.A.) and M.A. cars rejoined Unit	G.D.H.
	24/9/18		1. O.R. (R.A.M.C.) evacuated (sick)	G.D.H.

Army Form C. 2118.

WAR DIARY
INTELLIGENCE SUMMARY.
(Erase heading not required.)

Place	Date	Hour	Summary of Events and Information	Remarks and references to Appendices
LE BARQUE	27/9/18		1. O.R. (ASC) HT joined for duty	
			Established a Debouching Post for Walking wounded at H32 Central Sheet 57c.	G.D.H.
	30/9/18		Capt. & Q.M. McClahan evacuated (sick) to No 34 CCS	
			10. O.R. Evacuated on Leave	
			Unit moved from LE BARQUE and took over Main Dressing Stn, YPRES.	G.D.H.
			from 15 Field Ambulance	
			Capt. W. Craig. RAMC reported to O.C. 98 Field Ambulance for duty	
			2 Bearer Sub Divisions and 2 M.A. Cars reported to O.C. 48 Fd. Amb. for duty	
			2 Bearer Sub Divisions (HQ Fd Amb) attached to him until a/c	
			Divisional reserve	

C.D. Hindley Lt Col RAMC

Commanding 50 Field Ambulance

CONFIDENTIAL.

War Diary

of

Officer Commanding, 50th Field Ambulance

From 1st October 1918 to 31st October 1918.

(Volume 39)

Army Form C. 2118.

WAR DIARY
INTELLIGENCE SUMMARY.

(Erase heading not required.)

SHEET I.

Place	Date	Hour	Summary of Events and Information	Remarks and references to Appendices
YPRES	1/10/18		War Diary of C.C. 50 Field Ambulance for month of October 1918.	
			Unit moved from YPRES and established Main Dressing Station at METZ.	G.D.H.
			G.D. Hindley Lt. Col. RAMC Commanding 50 Field Ambulance	
METZ	2/10/18		1 O.R. (R.A.M.C.) joined for duty.	
			Lieut. W.M. RICHARDS - R.A.M.C. transferred to medical charge 1st Bgde. T.F.A.	
			Detaining Post (at H.Q. central dues syst) for walking wounded, handed over to 5th Division.	G.D.H.
			1 O.R. (A.S.C. M.T.) evacuated sick.	
	3/10/18		Lieut. E.L. BLACKNEY - M.O.R.C. - U.S.A. joined for duty	G.D.H.
	4/10/18		2 Revr. Subs - Divisions (49th 3rd Amb) attached to this unit as @ divisional Reserve, joined 46 F. Amb. for temporary duty.	G.D.H.
	6/10/18		Unit moved from METZ and formed Main Dressing Station at GOUZEAUCOURT on site previously occupied by 46 F. Amb. as advanced Dressing Station	G.D.H.
GOUZEAUCOURT	7/10/18		9 O.R. proceeded on leave.	G.D.H.

Army Form C. 2118.

SHEET II.

WAR DIARY
INTELLIGENCE SUMMARY.
(Erase heading not required.)

Instructions regarding War Diaries and Intelligence Summaries are contained in F. S. Regs., Part II. and the Staff Manual respectively. Title pages will be prepared in manuscript.

Place	Date	Hour	Summary of Events and Information	Remarks and references to Appendices
GOUZEAUCOURT	8/10/18		Capt. E.C. TREADGOLD - R.A.M.C. joined for duty.	G.D.H.
	9/10/18		1 O.R. (A.S.C. M.T) joined for duty. Unit moved from GOUZEAUCOURT and formed Main Dressing Station at VAUCELLES.	G.D.H.
			1 O.R. (R.A.M.C) evacuated (sick)	
			1 O.R. (R.A.M.C) evacuated (wounded).	
VAUCELLES	10/10/18	08.00	Unit moved from VAUCELLES and formed Main Dressing Station at ESNES.	G.D.H.
ESNES	10/10/18	14.00	Unit moved from ESNES and formed Main Dressing Station at LIGNY. Capt. E.C. TREADGOLD - R.A.M.C. transferred to 4.F. Amb. for duty.	G.D.H.
LIGNY	11/10/18		3rd Amb. moved to different site in LIGNY and formed Main Dressing Station.	G.D.H.
	12/10/18		1 O.R. proceeded on leave.	G.D.H.
	14/10/18		Capt. W. CRAIG - R.A.M.C. rejoined unit from temporary duty with 4.F. Amb. Field Ambulance commenced to function as Divisional Rest Station.	G.D.H.
	16/10/18		3. R.A.M.C. reinforcements joined for duty.	G.D.H.

Army Form C. 2118.

SHEET 711

WAR DIARY
—or—
INTELLIGENCE SUMMARY.
(Erase heading not required.)

Place	Date	Hour	Summary of Events and Information	Remarks and references to Appendices
LIGNY	18/10/18		{Lieut E.L. BRACKNEY - M.O.R.C. - U.S.A. took temporary medical charge of 1/1 Bn Herts Regt. during the absence on leave of Capt. R.W. MACLARAN - M.C. - R.A.M.C.	G.D.H.
	19/10/18		2 O.R. (R.A.M.C.) rejoined for duty.	G.D.H.
	21/10/18		1 O.R. proceeded on 4 days leave to PARIS.	G.D.H.
	22/10/18		9 O.R. proceeded on leave.	G.D.H.
			4 R.A.M.C. reinforcements joined for duty.	
	23/10/18		2 Bearer Sub-Divisions, 3 Horsed Ambulance Wagons and all available motor cars (except two) reported to C.O. 49th F. Amb. at A.D.S. for temporary duty.	G.D.H.
	25/10/18		1 O.R. (R.A.M.C.) rejoined for duty.	G.D.H.
			1 O.R. (R.A.M.C.) joined for duty.	
			Capt. E.C. MACKAY - R.A.M.C. reported to C.C. 49th Amb. for temporary duty.	
	27/10/18		Unit moved from LIGNY and formed Divl. Rest Station at BRIASTRE.	G.D.H.
			1 O.R. proceeded on leave.	
BRIASTRE	28/10/18		5 O.R. proceeded on leave.	G.D.H.

WAR DIARY
INTELLIGENCE SUMMARY.
(Erase heading not required.)

Army Form C. 2118.

SHEET IV

Place	Date	Hour	Summary of Events and Information	Remarks and references to Appendices
BRIASTRE	29/10/18		1 O.R. (R.A.M.C.) rejoined unit from hospital.	G.D.H.
	30/10/18		2 O.R. (R.A.M.C) evacuated (wounded).	G.D.H.
	31/10/18		nothing further to report.	G.D.H.

C.D. Hindley Lt.Col. R.A.M.C.
Commanding 50 Field Ambulance

CONFIDENTIAL.

M 38

140/3401

[Stamp: 50TH FIELD AMBULANCE]

[Stamp: COMMITTEE MEDICAL HIST]

War Diary

of

Officer Commanding, 50th Field Ambulance

From 1st November 1918 to 30th November 1918.

(Volume 40.)

Army Form C. 2118.

WAR DIARY
INTELLIGENCE SUMMARY.
(Erase heading not required.)

SHEET I.

Place	Date	Hour	Summary of Events and Information	Remarks and references to Appendices
BRIASTRE	4/11/18		War Diary of No. 50 Field Ambulance for month of November 1918.	
			Capt. W. CRAIG - R.A.M.C. reported to No. 48 F. Amb. for temporary duty.	G.D.H
				G.D. Hindley Lt.Col. R.A.M.C. Commanding 50 Field Ambulance
	5/11/18		All remaining M.Os, except one, reported to No. 49th F. Amb. for temporary duty. 8 O.R. proceeded on leave.	
			Capt. W. CRAIG - R.A.M.C. rejoined unit from temporary duty with 48 F.Amb. All motor and horsed Ambulances temporarily attached to 49 F. Amb. for duty, rejoined unit.	G.D.H
	6/11/18		Capt. E.C. MACKAY - R.A.M.C. rejoined unit from temporary duty with 48 F. Amb.	G.D.H
			Lieut E.L. BRACKNEY - M.O.R.C - U.S.A rejoined unit from temporary duty as M.O. i/c 1/1st Herts	
	8/11/18		Divl Rest Station at BRIASTRE Chateau handed over to 48 F. Amb. as from 12 noon. 1 O.R. proceeded on special leave to U.K.	G.D.H
BEAUVRAIN	9/11/18		Unit moved from BRIASTRE to BEAUVRAIN. Left 1-30 p.m. arrived 8-30 p.m. Unit moved from BEAUVRAIN to LOUVIGNIES. Left 8 a.m. arrived 10 a.m.	G.D.H

WAR DIARY
or
INTELLIGENCE SUMMARY.
(Erase heading not required.)

Army Form C. 2118.
SHEET VI

Place	Date	Hour	Summary of Events and Information	Remarks and references to Appendices
LOUVIGNIES	9/11/18		1/Lt. E.L. BRACKNEY - M.O.R.C. - U.S.A. took temporary medical charge of 17th B. Essex Regt.	G.D.H.
	11/11/18		Capt. E.C. MACKAY - R.A.M.C. took temporary medical charge of 34th Divl. T.E.O.	G.D.H
			1 O.R. proceeded on leave	
			Unit moved from LOUVIGNIES to BETHENCOURT. Left 9-45 a.m. arrived 3.30 p.m.	
BETHENCOURT	12/11/18		1 O.R. proceeded on special leave to U.K.	G.D.H.
	13/11/18		9 O.R. attended parade at CAUDRY for presentation medal ribands by Corps Commander	G.D.H.
	15/11/18		Unit inspected on parade by ADMS 34th Division	G.D.H.
	16/11/18		Capt. T.B. WATSON - R.A.M.C. and Lieut W.M. RICHARDS - R.A.M.C. transferred to D Dm.S IX Corps for duty	G.D.H.
	18/11/18		Capt. E.C. MACKAY - R.A.M.C. and 2 O.R. proceeded on leave	G.D.H.
	19/11/18		1/Lieut E.L. BRACKNEY - M.O.R.C. - U.S.A evacuated (sick) to No. 2 C.C.S. 2nd Amb. Car reported to M/O i/c 34th Return Group for temporary duty in replacement of a car from 34th M.A.C.	G.D.H.
	20/11/18		One section of Field Amb. paraded with 111th Inf. Bde. for inspection by Divl. Commander.	G.D.H.
	22/11/18		Division reviewed by G.O.C. at CAUDRY.	G.D.H.

Army Form C. 2118.

SHEET III

WAR DIARY
or
INTELLIGENCE SUMMARY.

(Erase heading not required.)

Instructions regarding War Diaries and Intelligence Summaries are contained in F. S. Regs., Part II. and the Staff Manual respectively. Title pages will be prepared in manuscript.

Place	Date	Hour	Summary of Events and Information	Remarks and references to Appendices
BETHENCOURT	25/11/18		1 O.R. (R.A.M.C) reported for duty.	G.D.H.
			1 O.R. (R.A.M.C) evacuated sick	
	23/11/18		Major C.J.B. WAY - M.C - R.A.M.C and 2 O.R. proceeded on leave.	G.D.H.
	24/11/18		1 O.R. (A.S.C. M.T.) evacuated (sick)	G.D.H.
	24/11/18		1 O.R. (R.A.M.C) evacuated (sick)	G.D.H.
	30/11/18		Capt. W. CRAIG - R.A.M.C took temporary medical charge of 10th Royal Fusiliers.	G.D.H.

C.D Hindley
Lt Col RAMC
Commanding 50 Field Ambulance

CONFIDENTIAL.

War Diary

of

Officer Commanding 50th Field Ambulance.

From 1st December 1918 to 31st December 1918.

Volume H

Army Form C. 2118.

WAR DIARY
or
INTELLIGENCE SUMMARY.
SHEET I.
(Erase heading not required.)

Instructions regarding War Diaries and Intelligence Summaries are contained in F. S. Regs., Part II. and the Staff Manual respectively. Title pages will be prepared in manuscript.

Place	Date	Hour	Summary of Events and Information	Remarks and references to Appendices
			War Diary of U.B. 50 Field Ambulance for month of December 1918.	
BETHENCOURT	1/12/18		2 O.R. proceeded on leave. J.R.Ray	
				Major Rowe I/c U.B. 50 Fd Ambulance
	2/12/18		Unit moved from BETHENCOURT to BERMERAIN. Left 0830 hrs. arrived 1330 hrs.	OBRs
BERMERAIN	3/12/18		Unit moved from BERMERAIN to ETH. Left 0830 hrs. arrived 1330 hrs.	OBRs
ETH	5/12/18		Capt. E. C. MACKAY - R.A.M.C. returned from leave to U.K.	OBRs
	6/12/18		Capt. W. CRAIG - R.A.M.C. and 3 O.R. proceeded on leave to U.K.	OBRs
	10/12/18		Orders received for Capt. W. CRAIG - R.A.M.C. to proceed home at once for Demobilization.	CWRs
			1 O.R. proceeded on leave to PARIS.	OBRs
	12/12/18		Major C.J.B.WAY - M.C. - R.A.M.C. returned from leave to U.K.	OBRs
			1 O.R. proceeded on Special Leave to U.K.	OBRs
	13/12/18		Capt. E. C. MACKAY - R.A.M.C. took temporary medical charge of 10 Royal Fusiliers	
	14/12/18		Unit moved from ETH to BETTRECHIES. Left 1145 hrs arrived 1500 hrs.	OBRs
BETTRECHIES	15/12/18		4 O.R. proceeded on leave to U.K.	OBRs

Army Form C. 2118.

WAR DIARY
or
INTELLIGENCE SUMMARY.   SHEET II

(Erase heading not required.)

Instructions regarding War Diaries and Intelligence Summaries are contained in F. S. Regs., Part II. and the Staff Manual respectively. Title pages will be prepared in manuscript.

Place	Date	Hour	Summary of Events and Information	Remarks and references to Appendices
BETTRECHIES	15/11/18		Unit moved from BETTRECHIES to LALONGUEVILLE. Left 1315 hrs. arrived 1700 hrs. ORW	
LALONGUEVILLE	16/11/18		Unit moved from LALONGUEVILLE to ELESMES. Left 0940 hrs arrived 1315 hrs. ORW	
ELESMES	18/11/18		Unit moved from ELESMES to BINCHE. Left 0945 hrs. arrived 1500 hrs. ORW	
BINCHE	19/11/18		Unit moved from BINCHE to PIETON. Left 0945 hrs arrived 1515 hrs. ORW	
PIETON	20/11/18		Unit moved from PIETON to JUMET (Hamendes). Left 0830 hrs. arrived 1445 hrs. ORW	
JUMET (Hamendes)	20/11/18		4 O.R. proceeded on leave to U.K. ORW	
			1 O.R. (R.A.M.C.) evacuated, sick.	
			4 O.R. proceeded to U.K. for demobilization ORW	
	23/11/18		4 O.R. proceeded to U.K. for demobilization ORW	
	24/11/18		4 O.R. proceeded to U.K. for demobilization ORW	
	25/11/18		3 O.R. proceeded to U.K. for demobilization ORW	
	26/11/18		2 O.R. proceeded to U.K. for demobilization ORW	
	27/11/18		2 O.R. proceeded to U.K. for demobilization ORW	
	29/11/18		6 O.R. proceeded on leave to U.K. ORW	

Army Form C. 2118.

WAR DIARY
or
INTELLIGENCE SUMMARY.
(Erase heading not required.)

SHEET III

Place	Date	Hour	Summary of Events and Information	Remarks and references to Appendices
JUMET (Hainault)	29/11/18		Lieut. Col. G. D. HINDLEY - M.C - R.A.M.C. proceeded on leave to PARIS and handed over command of 50 Field Amb. temporarily to Major C. J. B. WAY. M.C - R.A.M.C	
	30/11/18		Capt. & Q.Mr. M. W. COLAHAN - R.A.M.C. proceeded on leave to U.K.	
	2/12/18		Nothing further to report.	

W. Finlay
Major R.A.M.C
Commanding 50 Field Ambulance

CONFIDENTIAL. 37 DN 98/46

War Diary Box 2327 1495/90

of

Officer Commanding, 50th Field Ambulance.

From 1st January 1919 to 31st January 1919.

(Volume 42.)

WAR DIARY
INTELLIGENCE SUMMARY. (SHEET I)

Army Form C. 2118.

Place	Date	Hour	Summary of Events and Information	Remarks and references to Appendices
JUMET (HAMENDES)	5/1/19		War Diary of 66. S.of R.d Ambulance for month of January 1919.	
			Capt. E. L. F. NASH - M.C. - R.A.M.C. on duty.	
			(signed) Major Name a/Officer Commanding S.of R.d Ambulance	
	5/1/19		Capt. E C MACKAY - R.A.M.C. rejoined from temporary duty on No. 40 F. Ambulance. OKC	
	6/1/19		6 O.R. proceeded on leave U.K.	
	9/1/19		6 O.R. proceeded to U.K. for demobilization. C.B.	
	10/1/19		1 O.R. proceeded to U.K. for demobilization C.B.	
	15/1/19		6 O.R. proceeded on leave. C.B.A.	
	15/1/19		Capt. R.S. DREW - R.A.M.C. joined for duty. C.B.A.	
	16/1/19		Lieut. Col. G D HINDLEY - M.C. - R.A.M.C. returned from leave to PARIS and went on to nor on No. 8 C.C.S. HAY - M.C. - R.A.M.C. assumed command of S.of R.d Ambulance from Major C.T.B. WAY - M.C. - R.A.M.C.	
			G. D. Hindley Lt. Col. R.A.M.C. Commanding S.of R.d Ambulance	G.D.H.
	20/1/19		1 O.R. proceeded to U.K. for demobilization	G.D.H.
	20/1/19		6 O.R. proceeded on leave	G. D.H
	22/1/19		9 O.R. proceeded to U.K. for demobilization	G.D.H
	23/1/19		1 O.R. proceeded on Special leave to U.K.	G.D.H

Army Form C. 2118.

WAR DIARY
of
INTELLIGENCE SUMMARY. (SHEET II)
(Erase heading not required.)

Instructions regarding War Diaries and Intelligence Summaries are contained in F. S. Regs., Part II. and the Staff Manual respectively. Title pages will be prepared in manuscript.

Place	Date	Hour	Summary of Events and Information	Remarks and references to Appendices
JUMET (HAMENDES)	24/1/19		1 O.R. proceeded on leave to TROUVILLE	G.D.H.
	25/1/19		16 O.R. proceeded to U.K. for demobilization	G.D.H.
	28/1/19		8 O.R. proceeded to U.K. for demobilization	G.D.H.
	29/1/19		9 O.R. proceeded on leave	G.D.H.
	30/1/19		1 O.R. proceeded to U.K. for repatriation to U.S.A	G.D.H.
	31/1/19		1 O.R. proceeded on Special leave to U.K.	G.D.H.

C.D. Hindley Lieut Colonel
Commanding 50 Field Ambulance

CONFIDENTIAL.

War Diary

of

Officer Commanding 50th Field Ambulance

From 1st February 1919 to 28th February 1919.

(Volume 48).

Army Form C. 2118.

WAR DIARY
INTELLIGENCE SUMMARY. SHEET I.
(Erase heading not required.)

Instructions regarding War Diaries and Intelligence Summaries are contained in F. S. Regs., Part II. and the Staff Manual respectively. Title pages will be prepared in manuscript.

Place	Date	Hour	Summary of Events and Information	Remarks and references to Appendices
JUMET (HAMENDE)	3/2/19		War Diary of 26. 50 Field Ambulance for month of February 1919.	
	3/2/19		6 O.R. proceeded on leave.	G.D.H.
			G.D Hindley Lt.Col. R.A.M.C. Commanding 50 Field Ambulance	
	4/2/19		3 O.R. proceeded to U.K. for demobilization	G.D.H.
	5/2/19		1 O.R. proceeded on Special Leave.	G.D.H.
	7/2/19		3 O.R. proceeded to U.K. for demobilization.	G.D.H.
	10/2/19		10 O.R. proceeded on leave.	G.D.H.
	11/2/19		3 O.R. proceeded to U.K. for demobilization	G.D.H.
	12/2/19		3 O.R. proceeded to U.K. for demobilization	G.D.H.
	14/2/19		Captain R.S. DREW - R.A.M.C. took over medical charge of 37th Divl. Amm. Column	G.D.H.
	16/2/19		3 O.R. proceeded to U.K. for demobilization	G.D.H.
	17/2/19		1 O.R. proceeded on leave.	G.D.H.
	19/2/19		3 O.R. proceeded to U.K. for demobilization	G.D.H.
	22/2/19		3 O.R. proceeded to U.K. for demobilization	G.D.H.
	24/2/19		1 O.R. (R.A.S.C.) H.T. evacuated (sick)	G.D.H.
			1 O.R. proceeded on leave.	G.D.H.

Army Form C. 2118.

WAR DIARY
or
INTELLIGENCE SUMMARY. SHEET 11.

(Erase heading not required.)

Place	Date	Hour	Summary of Events and Information	Remarks and references to Appendices
JUMET (HAMENDES)	25/4/19		3 O.R. proceeded to U.K. for demobiligation.	G.D.H.
	28/4/19		3 O.R. proceeded to U.K. for demobiligation.	G.D.H.

G.D. Hindley Lt. Col. R.A.M.C.
Commanding 3 of ueed Ambulance

CONFIDENTIAL.

13 War Diary

of

Officer Commanding, 50th Field Ambulance.

From 1st March 1919 to 31st March 1919.

(Volume 44)

Army Form C. 2118.

WAR DIARY
or
INTELLIGENCE SUMMARY.
(Erase heading not required.)

SHEET 1.

Instructions regarding War Diaries and Intelligence Summaries are contained in F. S. Regs., Part II. and the Staff Manual respectively. Title pages will be prepared in manuscript.

Place	Date	Hour	Summary of Events and Information	Remarks and references to Appendices
JUMET (HAMENDE)			War Diary of 46. S.of Field Ambulance for month of March 1919	
	3/3/19		3 O.R. proceeded to U.K. for demobilization	G.D.H.
			C.D Hindley Lt. Col. R.A.M.C. Commanding 46 Field Ambulance	
	6/3/19		3 O.R. proceeded to U.K for demobilization	G.D.H.
	9/3/19		3 O.R. proceeded to U.K. for demobilization	G.D.H.
	10/3/19		3 O.R. proceeded on leave to U.K.	G.D.H.
	11/3/19		Ceased to take in sick, under instructions from A.D.M.S. 39th Div: - all sick, except emergencies, which are evacuated to C.C.S. in the usual manner, are from today, to be sent to 46th Fd Amb. for admission.	G.D.H.
	12/3/19		3 O.R. proceeded to U.K. for demobilization	G.D.H.
	13/3/19		2 O.R. proceeded on leave to U.K.	G.D.H
	15/3/19		4 O.R. proceeded to U.K. for demobilization	G.D.H.
			Major C.J.B. WAY - M.C. - R.A.M.C. proceeded on leave to U.K	
	18/3/19		3 O.R. proceeded to U.K. for demobilization	G.D.H.
	20/3/19		2 O.R. proceeded on leave to U.K	G.D.H.

Army Form C. 2118.

WAR DIARY
or
INTELLIGENCE SUMMARY.
(Erase heading not required.)

SHEET II

Instructions regarding War Diaries and Intelligence Summaries are contained in F. S. Regs., Part II. and the Staff Manual respectively. Title pages will be prepared in manuscript.

Place	Date	Hour	Summary of Events and Information	Remarks and references to Appendices
JUMET (NAMENDES)	21/3/19		2 O.R. Proceeded to U.K. for demobilization.	G.D.H.
	27/3/19		3 O.R. Proceeded on leave to U.K.	G.D.H.
	28/3/19		Captain R.H. LEIGH - M.C. - R.A.M.C. transferred to No. 20 C.C.S. for duty.	G.D.H.
			Lieut. M.C. MORALES - M.O.R.C. - U.S.A. joined for duty.	G.D.H.
	31/3/19		1 O.R. Proceeded to U.K. for demobilization	G.D.H.

G.D Hindley
Lieut. Col. R.A.M.C.
Commanding 50 Field Ambulance

VISION	Remaining		Admitted		Discharged		Duty		Transferred Rest S		Evacuated		at To-day.		Trench	
	S.	W.	S.	W.	S.	W.	S.	W.	S.	W.	S.	W.	S.	W.		

Unit.				OFFICERS.								Disease.	

SCABIES.

Remnd.

Admtd.

Lieut. Col. R.A.M.C.
Commanding 50th Field Ambulance

CONFIDENTIAL.

140/3050.

Vol 4 & 3 ceased

War Diary

of

Officer Commanding, 50th Field Ambulance.

From 1st April 1919 to 30th April 1919.

(Volume #5)

17 JUL 1919

50th FIELD AMBULANCE.

WAR DIARY
INTELLIGENCE SUMMARY

Army Form C. 2118.

Place	Date	Hour	Summary of Events and Information	Remarks and references to Appendices
JUMET (HAMENDES)	1/4/19		War Diary of No. 50th Field Ambulance for month of April 1919. Lieut M.G. MORALES - M.O.R.C. - U.S.A. transferred to American Base for demobilisation.	G.D.H.
			G.D. Hindley Lieut. Col. R.A.M.C. Commanding 50 Field Ambulance	
	13/4/19		1 O.R. proceeded to U.K. for demobilisation.	G.D.H.
	14/4/19		Capt. E.A. RUNTING - R.A.M.C. joined for duty	G.D.H.
	24/4/19		Capt. E.L.F. NASH - M.C. - R.A.M.C. transferred to 20th C.C.S. for duty.	G.D.H.
	24/4/19		Capt. (a/major) C.J.B. WAY - M.C. - R.A.M.C. evacuated (sick) to Base.	G.D.H.
	30/4/19		Capt. E.A. RUNTING - R.A.M.C. transferred to 20th C.C.S. for duty.	G.D.H.
	30/4/19		Cadre of 50 Field Ambulance entrains at CHARLEROI Station for transfer to the United Kingdom (PREES HEATH)	G.D.H.

G.D. Hindley Lieut. Col. R.A.M.C.
Commanding 50 Field Ambulance

www.ingramcontent.com/pod-product-compliance
Lightning Source LLC
Chambersburg PA
CBHW080914230426
43667CB00015B/2673